—STAN TOLER—

GENERAL EDITOR

THE ULTIMATE

KNOWLEDGE

CHALLENGE

HARVEST HOUSE PUBLISHERS
EUGENE, OREGON

Cover by Jason Gabbert Design

The Ultimate Bible Knowledge Challenge
Copyright © 2018 by Meadow's Edge Group, LLC
Published by Harvest House Publishers
Eugene, Oregon 97408
www.harvesthousepublishers.com

ISBN 978-0-7369-7416-5 (pbk.)
ISBN 978-0-7369-7417-2 (eBook)

Library of Congress Cataloging-in-Publication Data

Names: Toler, Stan, author.
Title: The ultimate Bible knowledge challenge / Stan Toler (general editor).
Description: Eugene : Harvest House Publishers, 2018.
Identifiers: LCCN 2018009509 (print) | LCCN 2018019983 (ebook) | ISBN 9780736974172 (ebook) | ISBN 9780736974165 (pbk.)
Subjects: LCSH: Bible--Miscellanea.
Classification: LCC BS615 (ebook) | LCC BS615 .U48 2018 (print) | DDC 220--dc23
LC record available at https://lccn.loc.gov/2018009509

Printed in the United States of America

18 19 20 21 22 23 24 25 26 / BP-GL / 10 9 8 7 6 5 4 3 2 1

Contents

PART 2
Things We Say from the Bible

PART 3
Bible Knowledge Challenge

PART 4
Essential Bible Verses

Increase Your Knowledge of the Bible

If you think about the Bible's impact on our world and on human history, you shouldn't be surprised you're interested in exploring and learning more about it. Whether you're an avid reader or a "Sunday browser," you have a sense of the Bible's importance. God's Word continues to be the No. 1 bestseller. More than 100 million copies are sold globally each year, and countless others are distributed for free in countries open to and closed to its availability.

By understanding the Bible better, you can also recognize and appreciate the unspoken influence it has on our everyday lives.

What increases our interest in and devotion to the greatest book of all time? Despite a plethora of theories, reasons, and continued debate, for most of us the Bible has a proven track record. Millions of people around the globe have encountered the Scriptures, and these teachings have enriched and transformed lives, as well as shaped the way we think about our world.

Some people first encountered the Bible at a young age. Others discovered it later in life, perhaps because of a personal crisis or as a next step on a spiritual journey.

What is your motivation for reading this book right now? Is it a self-challenge to learn just how much you know (or don't know yet) about the Bible? Or are you simply thinking it will be fun to learn something new?

Whatever your reason, I hope this book will help you appreciate the Bible's impact around the world and in your own home. We are all blessed to have our lives changed by the Bible's ultimate truths.

Stan Toler, GENERAL EDITOR

PART 1

Bible Knowledge and Learning

Important Facts and Dates in Compiling the Books of the Bible

The Ten Commandments delivered to Moses	1400 BC
Completion of Hebrew manuscripts that would become the 39 Old Testament books	500–400 BC
Completion of all manuscripts that would make up the 27 books of the New Testament	First century AD
Completion of the Septuagint, a Greek translation (from the Hebrew) of all 39 books of the Old Testament canon, and the 14 books of the Apocrypha	Third and second centuries BC
Athanasius, bishop of Alexandria, identifies the 27 books of the New Testament	AD 367
Council of Hippo affirms the canon of the New Testament	AD 393

The Life of Abraham

- From the Ur of the Chaldees to Haran—the death of Abram's father, Terah (Genesis 11:31-32)

- From Haran to Shechem—Abram builds an altar (Genesis 12:1-7)

- From Shechem to Bethel—Abram offers sacrifices to God (Genesis 12:8)

- From Bethel to Egypt—Abram denies Sarai is his wife (Genesis 12:10-16)

- From Egypt to Bethel—Abram offers prayers (Genesis 13:1-4)

- From Bethel to Hebron—Abram builds an altar and offers sacrifice (Genesis 13:18)

- From Hebron to Hobah—Abram rescues Lot (Genesis 14:1-16)

- From Hobah to Hebron—Ishmael is born, God changes Abram's name to Abraham and his wife's to Sarah, three angels give promise of a son, Sodom is destroyed (Genesis 14:16–19:25)

- From Hebron to Gerar—Isaac is born and presented to Abraham (Genesis 21:1-21)

- From Gerar to Beersheba—Abraham makes a covenant with Abimelech (Genesis 21:31-34)

- From Beersheba to Mount Moriah—Abraham is willing to sacrifice Isaac but is spared doing so at the last moment (Genesis 22:1-8)

- From Mount Moriah to Beersheba—Abraham and his young men return to Beersheba (Genesis 22:19)

- From Beersheba to Hebron—the death of Abraham's wife, Sarah (Genesis 23:1-2; 19-20)

- From Hebron to Beersheba—the death of Abraham at 175 years of age (Genesis 25:7-8)

Twenty Miracles Associated with Moses

1. Moses's staff turns into a serpent and then back into a staff (Exodus 4:2-4).

2. Moses's hand becomes leprous and then returns to normal (Exodus 4:6-7).

3. Aaron's staff becomes a serpent and swallows up the sorcerers' rods that had become serpents (Exodus 7:10-12).

4. God hides the Hebrews with a cloud (Exodus 14:19-20).

5. The Red Sea parts and the sea bottom becomes dry land (Exodus 14:21).

6. The waters of the Red Sea return and drown the Egyptian army (Exodus 14:23-28).

7. Bitter waters at Marah are made sweet (Exodus 15:23-25).

8. Hebrews are fed with quail (Exodus 16:11-13).

9. Hebrews are fed with manna (Exodus 16:14-24).

10. Moses strikes a rock in Horeb to produce water for the Hebrews (Exodus 17:1-6).

11. Fire from the Lord consumes a burnt offering (Leviticus 9:22-24).

12. Miriam made leprous and then healed (Numbers 12).

13. Complaining Hebrews burned up by fire from the Lord until Moses intercedes (Numbers 11:1-2).

14. Fire from the Lord consumes 250 men who treated the Lord with contempt (Numbers 16:16-18,35).

15. Earth opens up and swallows Korah and his men (Numbers 16:28-33).

16. A plague that kills 14,700 is stopped by making an offering of incense (Numbers 16:46-50).

17. Aaron's staff grows, buds, and blossoms (Numbers 17).

18. Moses strikes a rock twice to bring forth water (Numbers 20:1-11).

19. Moses makes a brass serpent and puts it on a pole. Those bitten by venomous snakes live when they look at the serpent (Numbers 21:5-9).

20. Moses appears on the Mount of Transfiguration with Jesus (Luke 9:28-36).

More About Moses

- Family:

  > Father: Amram; Mother: Jochebed (Exodus 6:20)

  > From the tribe of Levi (Exodus 2:1)

  > Brother: Aaron (Exodus 4:14)

  > Sister: Miriam (Exodus 15:20)

- Early Life:

  > His birth (Exodus 2:2)

  > Adopted by the Pharaoh's daughter and named Moses (Exodus 2:10)

- Youth and Adulthood—kills an Egyptian and flees to Midian (Exodus 2:11-15)

- At Midian—marries Zipporah, a priest's daughter (Exodus 2:16-25)

- God's call—sees burning bush and hears God's call but makes excuses; God promises divine and human help (Exodus 3:1-4,16-18)

- Return to Egypt—demands that a stubborn Pharaoh free the people of Israel; God sends plagues; the Passover is established; Pharaoh frees the Israelites (Exodus 4:29–12:32)

- The Exodus from Egypt—Pharaoh pursues the Israelites; the Israelites cross the Red Sea; Moses sings the Song of Moses; God provides for the Israelites (Exodus 12:33–18:27)

- At Mount Sinai—ascends the mountain three times and makes a covenant with God; receives the Ten

Commandments and the rest of the Law; responds to the gold calf (Exodus 19–40)

- Journey from Sinai to Kadesh Barnea—the pillar of the cloud appears; the people complain; 70 elders are appointed (Numbers 10:11–12:15)

- At Kadesh Barnea—the spies report on the promised land; the people rebel, resulting in God's wrath; Amalek defeats Israel (Numbers 13:26–14:45)

- Forty years in the wilderness—God declares the people will wander; rebellion breaks out (Numbers 14:33–16:50)

- Return to Kadesh Barnea—the death of Miriam, Moses's sister; the people complain over lack of water; Moses sins (Numbers 20:1-13)

- Final days—Moses's farewell address and blessing; Moses views the promised land; Moses's death (Deuteronomy 32:1–34:6)

- Appearance after death—Moses and Elijah appear at Jesus's transfiguration (Matthew 17:2-3)

The Ten Commandments

Exodus 20:2-17

1. I am the LORD your God, who brought you out of Egypt, out of the land of slavery. You shall have no other gods before me.

2. You shall not make for yourself an image in the form of anything in heaven above or on the earth beneath or in the waters below. You shall not bow down to them or worship them; for I, the LORD your God, am a jealous God, punishing the children for the sin of the parents to the third and fourth generation of those who hate me, but showing love to a thousand generations of those who love me and keep my commandments.

3. You shall not misuse the name of the LORD your God, for the LORD will not hold anyone guiltless who misuses his name.

4. Remember the Sabbath day by keeping it holy. Six days you shall labor and do all your work, but the seventh day is a Sabbath to the LORD your God. On it, you shall not do any work, neither you, nor your son or daughter, nor your male or female servant, nor your animals, nor any foreigner residing in your towns. For in six days the LORD made the heavens and the earth, the sea, and all that is in them, but he rested on the seventh day. Therefore the LORD blessed the Sabbath day and made it holy.

5. Honor your father and your mother, so you may live long in the land the LORD your God is giving you.

6. You shall not murder.

7. You shall not commit adultery.

8. You shall not steal.

9. You shall not give false testimony against your neighbor.

10. You shall not covet your neighbor's house. You shall not covet your neighbor's wife, or his male or female servant, his ox or donkey, or anything that belongs to your neighbor.

Food-Related Miracles in the Bible

- God sends manna to the Israelites to eat daily, except on the Sabbath (Exodus 16:14-33).

- God sends quail for the Israelites to eat (Numbers 11:4-6,31-34).

- The widow of Zarephath's flour and oil supply holds steady (1 Kings 17:9,14-16).

- Elijah is fed by ravens (1 Kings 17:2-6).

- A widow's oil is multiplied (2 Kings 4:2-7).

- A deadly stew is cured with flour at Gilgal (2 Kings 4:38-41).

- One hundred men are fed with 20 loaves at Gilgal (2 Kings 4:42-44).

- A miraculous catch of fish is made (Luke 5:4-11).

- Jesus turns water into wine (John 2:1-11).

- Jesus feeds 5000 men, plus women and children (Matthew 14:13-21; Mark 6:30-44; Luke 9:10-17; John 6:1-13).

- Jesus feeds 4000 (Matthew 15:32-38; Mark 8:1-9).

- Jesus curses a fig tree (Matthew 21:18-19; Mark 11:12-14).

- Israelites, under the command of Joshua, cross on dry ground (Joshua 3:15-17).

- Elijah and Elisha cross the Jordan on dry ground (2 Kings 2:8).

- Elisha crosses on dry ground by himself (2 Kings 2:14).

- God heals Naaman of leprosy by having him bathe in the Jordan's waters (2 Kings 5:1-14).

- Elisha makes an iron axhead float (2 Kings 6:1-6).

Isaiah's Prophecies of the Messiah

Prophecy	Reference	Fulfillment
Spoke in parables	Isaiah 6:9-10	Matthew 13:13-15
Born of a virgin	Isaiah 7:14	Matthew 1:18
Ministered in Galilee	Isaiah 9:1-2	Matthew 4:12-17
Healed the blind	Isaiah 35:5	John 9:1-7
Healed the deaf	Isaiah 35:5	Mark 7:32-35
Healed the lame	Isaiah 35:6	Matthew 15:30
Had compassion for the poor	Isaiah 42:3	Matthew 11:4-5
A light to the Gentiles	Isaiah 42:6	Luke 2:28-32
Sent by God	Isaiah 48:16	John 7:29
Came to glorify God	Isaiah 49:3	John 17:1
Grieved over the Jews' unbelief	Isaiah 49:4	Luke 19:41-42
His face beaten and spat upon	Isaiah 50:6	Matthew 26:67
His back whipped	Isaiah 50:6	Matthew 27:26
Shed his blood for all	Isaiah 52:15	Revelation 1:5
Rejected by his own people	Isaiah 53:3	John 1:11
Suffered for others	Isaiah 53:4-5	Matthew 8:16-17
Oppressed and afflicted	Isaiah 53:7	Matthew 27:27-31
Silent when accused	Isaiah 53:7	Matthew 26:62-63
Buried with the rich	Isaiah 53:9	Matthew 27:57-60
Suffered willingly	Isaiah 53:11	John 12:27
Gave up his life to save humanity	Isaiah 53:12	Luke 23:46
Crucified with sinners	Isaiah 53:12	Matthew 27:38
Preached the good news	Isaiah 61:1-2	Luke 4:17-22

Fifteen Miracles Associated with Elisha

1. Parting of the Jordan (2 Kings 2:14)

2. Healing of the water (2 Kings 2:21)

3. Curse of the bears (2 Kings 2:24)

4. Filling of the valley with water (2 Kings 3:17)

5. Deception of the Moabites (2 Kings 3:22)

6. Miracle of the jars of oil (2 Kings 4:4)

7. Resurrection of the Shunammite's son (2 Kings 4:34)

8. Curing of a deadly stew with flour (2 Kings 4:41)

9. Feeding 100 men with 20 loaves of barley bread (2 Kings 4:42-43)

10. Healing of Naaman (2 Kings 5:13-14)

11. Cursing Gehazi with leprosy (2 Kings 5:26-27)

12. The floating iron axhead (2 Kings 6:5-6)

13. Striking the Syrian army with blindness and then restoring their sight (2 Kings 6:18-20)

14. Deceiving the Syrians with the sound of chariots (2 Kings 7:1-6)

15. Resurrection of a man touched by Elisha's bones (2 Kings 13:20-21)

Bible Characters Raised from the Dead

- By Elijah: the son of the Zarephath widow (1 Kings 17:17-22)

- By Elisha: the son of the Shunammite woman (2 Kings 4:32-35)

- By Elisha: a man whose body touches Elisha's bones (2 Kings 13:20-21)

- By Jesus: the daughter of Jairus, a synagogue ruler (Luke 8:41-42,49-55)

- By Jesus: Lazarus, brother of Mary and Martha of Bethany (John 11:1-44)

- Upon the death and resurrection of Jesus: many saints rose from the dead (Matthew 27:50-53)

- By God the Father: Jesus Christ (Matthew 28:5-8; Mark 16:6; Luke 24:5-6)

- By Peter: a seamstress named Tabitha or Dorcas (Acts 9:36-41)

- By Paul: a young man named Eutychus (Acts 20:9-10)

What Believers Are Called in the Bible

- "Believers" (1 Timothy 4:12)

- "Ye blessed of my Father" (Matthew 25:34 KJV)

- "Brothers and sisters" (Acts 12:17)

- "Called to belong to Jesus Christ" (Romans 1:6)

- "Children of God" (John 1:12; Philippians 2:15; 1 John 3:1-2; John 11:52; 1 John 3:10)

- "Children of light" (Ephesians 5:8)

- "Children of the living God" (Romans 9:26)

- "Children of the Most High" (Luke 6:35)

- "Children of the promise" (Romans 9:8)

- "Children of the resurrection" (Luke 20:36)

- "Chosen people" (1 Peter 2:9)

- "Christians" (Acts 11:26)

- "Co-heirs with Christ" (Romans 8:17)

- "Dear brothers and sisters" (1 Corinthians 15:58; James 2:5)

- "Faithful brothers and sisters in Christ" (Colossians 1:2)

- "Fellow citizens with God's people" (Ephesians 2:19)

- "God's chosen people" (Colossians 3:12)

- "Heirs of God" (Romans 8:17)

- "Heirs of promise" (Hebrews 6:17 KJV)

- "Heirs together with Israel" (Ephesians 3:6)
- "Holy nation" (1 Peter 2:9)
- "Holy priesthood" (1 Peter 2:5)
- "Instruments for special purposes" (2 Timothy 2:21)
- "Light of the world" (Matthew 5:14)
- "Members of Christ" (1 Corinthians 6:15)
- "Obedient children" (1 Peter 1:14)
- "Objects of his mercy" (Romans 9:23)
- "People holy to the Lord" (Deuteronomy 14:2)
- "People of God" (Hebrews 4:9; 1 Peter 2:10)
- "People of the kingdom" (Matthew 13:38)
- "People of the light" (Luke 16:8)
- "Priests to serve his God and Father" (Revelation 1:6)
- "Royal priesthood" (1 Peter 2:9)
- "Salt of the earth" (Matthew 5:13)
- "Slaves to righteousness" (Romans 6:18)
- "The godly" (2 Peter 2:9)
- "The Lord's freed person" (1 Corinthians 7:22)
- "Those the Lord has rescued" (Isaiah 51:11)
- "Those who will inherit salvation" (Hebrews 1:14)

Timeline of David's Life

- Early years—Samuel anoints David king; serves as harpist for King Saul (1 Samuel 16:1-23; 17:15)

- Between years (Gibeah and Jerusalem)—David is given a high rank in Saul's army; Saul becomes jealous of David and twice attempts to kill him (1 Samuel 18:1–19:10)

- From Gibeah to Ramah to Naioth to Gibeah—David flees to Samuel the prophet at Ramah; returns to Gibeah and Saul's son Jonathan alerts him of his father's plan to kill David (1 Samuel 19:18-21; 20:42)

- From Gibeah to Nob to Gath—Ahimelech gives David consecrated bread and the sword of Goliath; David feigns insanity in Gath (1 Samuel 21:1-15)

- From Gath to Adullam to Mizpah to the forest of Hereth to Keilah—removes his parents from danger in Mizpah; fights the Philistines in Keilah (1 Samuel 22:1–23:5)

- From Keilah to the Desert of Ziph to the Desert of Maon to En Gedi to the Desert of Maon—makes a covenant with Jonathan in Ziph; spares Saul's life in En Gedi (1 Samuel 23:13–24:22)

- From the Desert of Maon to Carmel—meets and marries Abigail, Nabal's widow; again spares Saul's life (1 Samuel 25–26)

- From the Desert of Ziph to Gath to Ziklag to Gath—conquers Geshurites, Girzites, and Amalekites (1 Samuel 27:1-9)

- From Gath to Aphek to Ziklag to the south—finds Ziklag ravaged by the Amalekites: travels south to recover the property and people of Ziklag; returns to Ziklag (1 Samuel 29:9–30:26)

- From Ziklag to Hebron—anointed king of Israel following the death of Saul and Jonathan (2 Samuel 5:1-3)

- From Hebron to Jerusalem to Baal Perazim to Jerusalem—drives Philistines out of Baal Perazim and returns to Jerusalem (2 Samuel 5:1-21)

- From Jerusalem to Rephaim—defeats Philistines from Rephaim to Gibeon and Gezer (2 Samuel 5:22-25)

- From Jerusalem to Baalah to Gibeah—went to bring the ark of the covenant back to Jerusalem, but it is left on Obed-Edom's threshing floor (2 Samuel 6:2-11)

- From Jerusalem to the house of Obed-Edom—brings the ark of the covenant back to Jerusalem (2 Samuel 6:12-23)

- From Jerusalem to Metheg Ammah to Moab to Zobah to the Valley of Salt—places Moab under his control; conquers Hadadezer in Zobah; kills 18,000 Edomites in the Valley of Salt (2 Samuel 8:1-13)

- From Jerusalem to Helam—conquers the Arameans (2 Samuel 10:17-19)

- Jerusalem—sins with Bathsheba (2 Samuel 11)

- From Jerusalem to Rabbah—inhabitants of Rabbah are treated with cruelty (2 Samuel 12:29-31)

- From Jerusalem to Mahanaim—flees to Mahanaim following his son Absalom's coup; returns to Jerusalem and regains the throne after Absalom's death (2 Samuel 15–19)

- From Jerusalem—battles with the Philistines, places unknown (2 Samuel 21:15-22)

- Jerusalem—instructs his son and successor, Solomon (1 Kings 2:1-11)

David's Offspring

First Chronicles 3:1-9 lists 19 of David's sons by name and also reports that David had many other sons by his concubines, as well as a daughter named Tamar. (*Editor's note:* It's also likely he had many other daughters.) Following is a list of David's sons named in the Bible:

1. Amnon, by Ahinoam of Jezreel

2. Daniel, by Abigail of Carmel

3. Absalom, by Maacah (daughter of King Talmai of Geshur)

4. Adonijah, by Haggith

5. Shephatiah, by Abital

6. Ithream, by Eglah

7. Shammua, by Bathsheba

8. Shobab, by Bathsheba

9. Nathan, by Bathsheba

10. Solomon, by Bathsheba

11. Ibhar

12. Elishua

13. Eliphelet (his first son with this name)

14. Nogah

15. Nepheg

16. Japhia

17. Elishama

18. Eliada

19. Eliphelet (his second son with this name)

The Life of Judah

- Judah was one of the 12 sons of Jacob (Israel).

- The name Judah means "to praise."

- Judah's mother was Leah, one of Jacob's two wives. She also gave birth to Reuben, Simeon, Levi, Issachar, and Zebulun. His father's other wife was Rachel.

- Judah was the patriarch of one of the 12 tribes of Israel. The region of Israel that included the city of Jerusalem was named after Judah.

- The southern kingdom that came into existence after Israel divided into two kingdoms was called Judah.

- In the book of Genesis, Judah emerges as a leader in his family.

- Judah was instrumental in saving the life of his brother Joseph, whose brothers plotted to throw Joseph in a pit and leave him to die. Judah persuaded his brothers to instead sell Joseph to a passing group of Midianite merchants (Genesis 37:26-28).

- The Gospel of Matthew traces the ancestry of Joseph, the earthly father of Jesus, back to Judah.

- In Jacob's blessing of his 12 sons (see Genesis 49), he called Judah a "lion's cub" (verse 9) and said that his hand would be on the neck of his enemies, and that his brothers would praise him (verse 8).

Twelve Important Married Couples of the Bible

1. Adam and Eve

2. Abraham and Sarah

3. Isaac and Rebekah

4. Jacob and Rachel

5. Boaz and Ruth

6. Elkanah and Hannah

7. David and Bathsheba

8. Ahab and Jezebel

9. Joseph and Mary

10. Zechariah and Elizabeth

11. Ananias and Sapphira

12. Aquila and Priscilla

Solomon's Words of Wisdom and Great Accomplishments

The son of King David and Bathsheba, Solomon was loved by God. Despite the efforts of his half brother Adonijah to take the throne, Solomon became king over Israel with the support of his father.

When God came to Solomon in a vision and asked what he wanted, the king requested "a discerning heart" (1 Kings 3:9) to rule his people. Because Solomon asked wisely, God gave him wisdom, understanding, and the wealth and honor he had *not* requested. Solomon built the Lord's temple with the aid of Hiram, Tyre's king. Solomon dedicated the temple with a beautiful prayer and benediction (1 Kings 8:22-61).

While Solomon made more than his share of bad decisions during his monarchy (some of which led to the division of Israel into two kingdoms after his death), his words of wisdom are prominent in the Bible. Solomon is often credited with:

- Psalms 72 and 127

- The first 29 chapters of the book of Proverbs (Agur and Lemuel wrote chapters 30 and 31)

- The Song of Solomon (or the Song of Songs)

- The book of Ecclesiastes

- Possibly even the book of Job

Solomon's Reign and the Early History of Israel

Included in the Bible are 12 books called "history books." You can read about King Solomon and many other amazing people in these books:

- Joshua: The Israelites capture and settle the promised land of Canaan.

- Judges: Israel goes through cycles of sin, suffering, and salvation.

- Ruth: A loyal daughter-in-law portrays God's faithfulness, love, and care.

- 1 Samuel: Israel's twelve tribes unite under a king.

- 2 Samuel: David becomes Israel's greatest king, but with major flaws.

- 1 Kings: Israel divides into rival northern and southern nations.

- 2 Kings: Both Jewish nations are destroyed for their disobedience to God.

- 1 Chronicles: King David's reign is detailed and analyzed.

- 2 Chronicles: the history of Israel—from Solomon through division to destruction.

- Ezra: Spiritual renewal begins after the Jews return from exile.

- Nehemiah: Returning Jewish exiles rebuild the broken walls of Jerusalem.

- Esther: A beautiful Jewish girl becomes queen and then saves fellow Jews from slaughter.

The Meaning of a Nazirite

The word *Nazirite* (or *Nazarite*) comes from a Hebrew word meaning "separated" or "consecrated." A Nazirite was someone who was separated from the general Hebrew population and devoted completely to God.

The conditions of the Nazirite vow are in Numbers 6:1-8. In that passage, God directs Moses to tell the Israelites, both men and women, about the vow.

Specifically, the vow requires that Nazirites:

- Must abstain from consumption of alcohol and from any products of the grapevine, including vinegar, grape juice, grapes, grape seeds, grape skins, and raisins

- Must not cut their hair but let it grow long

- Must not touch or even go near a dead body, even that of a close family member

Nazirite vows were usually kept for one to three months, but Samson was a Nazirite from the time of his birth until his death (Judges 13:7). At the end of the period of the vow, the Nazirite was required to burn his (or her) shaven hair and present specific offerings to the Lord (Numbers 6:10-21).

The Judges of Israel

- Othniel—Caleb's brother, Othniel, delivered Israel from the king of Mesopotamia and judged Israel for 40 years (Judges 3:7-11).

- Ehud—He was the second judge of Israel, who subdued the oppressive Moabites (Judges 3:12-30).

- Shamgar—He fought bravely against the Philistines and killed 600 Philistine soldiers with an oxgoad (Judges 3:31).

- Deborah—She was Israel's only female judge and prophetess. She held court under a palm tree. Deborah called Barak to lead warriors into battle against the Canaanite army commander, Sisera (Judges 4–5).

- Gideon—He was the fifth judge of Israel, whom God raised up to lead his nation against the Midianites (Judges 6–8).

- Abimelech—He was a son of Gideon by his concubine. He killed all but one of his brothers and was made king in Shechem (Judges 9).

- Tola—He judged Israel for 23 years (Judges 10:1-2).

- Jair—He was the eighth judge of Israel, who led the nation for 22 years (Judges 10:3-5).

- Jephthah—The ninth judge of Israel, Jephthah the Gileadite, was Gilead's son by a prostitute (Judges 10:6–12:7).

- Ibzan—The tenth judge of Israel, Ibzan of Bethlehem led Israel for seven years and had 30 sons and 30 daughters (Judges 12:8-10).

- Elon—He judged Israel for ten years (Judges 12:11-12).

- Abdon—He was the twelfth judge of Israel, who led the nation for eight years (Judges 12:13-15).

- Samson—He was the thirteenth judge of Israel; from the time of his conception he was supposed to follow a Nazirite vow (Judges 13–16).

- Eli—He was the high priest in Shiloh, where the ark of the covenant rested for a time. He rebuked Hannah for being drunk when she prayed for God to give her a child. Eli judged Israel for 40 years (1 Samuel 4:18).

- Samuel—Samuel was born after his mother, Hannah, petitioned God to give her a child and promised to give him up to God's service in return (1 Samuel 1:1-22). Samuel spoke out against the wickedness of Eli's sons (1 Samuel 3:11-14). Samuel led the Israelites to repent of their idolatry, and he judged Israel throughout his life (1 Samuel 7:15).

The Life of Noah

- Early years: The Bible is silent about Noah's early life. The first time he is mentioned (when God calls him to build the ark and prepare his family for the destruction of the world), he is 600 years old. Noah was the great-great-grandson of Methuselah, who many believe lived longer than any man (Genesis 5:25-27). He was the great-grand-son of Enoch, the man who "walked faithfully with God" for 300 years before he was taken to heaven without dying (Genesis 5:22-24; Hebrews 11:5). He was the son of Lamech (Genesis 5:28-29).

- His family: Noah was married and had three sons—Shem, Ham, and Japheth. The name of Noah's wife is not mentioned in the Bible. She is referred to only as Noah's wife (Genesis 6:18; 7:7,13; 8:16,18).

- His call: Noah lived when humans had fallen so far into wickedness that God decided to destroy the world and start over (Genesis 6:6-7). God called Noah to build an enormous boat—the ark—to be a temporary home for him, his family, and a certain number of each member of the animal kingdom (Genesis 6:9–7:5). Even though what God commanded him to do must have seemed strange and humanly impossible, and even though unbelievers around him must have scoffed, Noah followed God's instructions faithfully and without hesitation.

- The flood: After Noah completed the ark, gathered all the animals, and entered the ark with his family—his wife, three sons, and their wives—God closed the great boat's doors and sent the flood that wiped out every living thing on earth (Genesis 7:16-23). The people and the animals stayed on the ark for several months before the boat came to rest among the mountains of Ararat (Genesis 8:4).

- Post-flood: After leaving the ark, Noah built an altar and offered God a sacrifice (Genesis 8:20). God instructed Noah and his family to begin repopulating the earth (Genesis 9:1). Noah planted a vineyard and, unfortunately, became drunk (Genesis 9:20-21). Noah lived 350 years after the flood and died at the ripe old age of 950 (Genesis 9:28).

What the Bible Says About Obedience

- It is part of our walk with God (Genesis 6:9).

- It is necessary to overcome our enemies (Exodus 23:22).

- It is key to God's blessing and a long life for ourselves and our families (Deuteronomy 4:39-40).

- It is necessary for those who wish to claim God's promises (Deuteronomy 6:18).

- It is necessary for those who desire to follow God (2 Kings 18:6).

- Obedience should be done wholeheartedly (2 Chronicles 31:21).

- Obedience blesses those who delight in it (Psalm 112:1).

- Obedience is a decision that believers make (Psalm 119:30).

- It must be done without hesitation (Psalm 119:60).

- It comes from the heart (Psalm 119:112).

- Obedience is key to eternal life (John 8:51).

- Obedience should be motivated by our love for God (John 14:15).

- Jesus demonstrated obedience perfectly (John 14:31).

- It is more important to obey God than men (Acts 5:29).

- Obedience results in a clear conscience (Acts 23:1).

- We who are in Christ are created for obedience (Ephesians 2:10).

- It should be done even when no one is watching (Philippians 2:12).

- It is motivated by faith (Hebrews 11:7).

- Obedience is the result of a changed heart (1 Peter 1:14).

- It is proof that God's Spirit is really within us (1 John 3:24).

- Obedience is not a burden to those who love God (1 John 5:3).

- Abraham's servant—He prayed for success in finding a wife for Isaac (Genesis 24:12).

- Jacob—He prayed for God's protection (Genesis 32:9-12).

- Moses—He prayed for mercy (Exodus 32:11-13,31-32; Deuteronomy 9:26-29).

- Moses—He prayed to know God and to see his glory (Exodus 33:12-18).

- Manoah—He prayed for guidance in raising his son, Samson (Judges 13:8).

- Hannah—She prayed to exalt God with thanksgiving and praise (1 Samuel 2:1-10).

- Elijah—He prayed for vindication and proof of God's power (1 Kings 18:36-37).

- Hezekiah—He prayed for deliverance from enemies (2 Kings 19:15-19).

- Solomon—He prayed for forgiveness of sins for Israel (2 Chronicles 6:21).

- Ezra—He prayed to confess his people's sin (Ezra 9:6-15).

- Jeremiah—He prayed to complain (Jeremiah 20:7-18).

- Daniel—He prayed with thanksgiving for help (Daniel 6:10-11).

- Daniel—He prayed to confess his people's sin (Daniel 9:9-19).

- Jonah—He prayed for restoration (Jonah 2:1-9).

- Jesus—He prayed for forgiveness for his enemies (Luke 23:34).

- Jesus—He prayed for himself, for the disciples, and for all believers (John 17).

- Apostles—They prayed for guidance in selecting Judas's replacement (Acts 1:24-25).

- Apostles—They prayed for the bold proclamation of the gospel, with miracles (Acts 4:29-30).

- Stephen—He prayed and asked the Lord to receive his spirit and to forgive his killers (Acts 7:59-60).

- This special box is distinguished from any other chest or coffer, with titles such as the "ark of God" (1 Samuel 3:3), the "ark of the covenant" (Joshua 3:6), or the "ark of the testimony" (Exodus 25:22 KJV).

- It was made of acacia—or shittim (KJV)—wood, was 2.5 cubits long, and was covered inside and out in the purest gold (Exodus 25:10-11).

- Its upper lid, also known as the mercy seat, was surrounded with a rim of gold, and on each of the two sides were two gold rings in which were placed two gold-covered poles by which the ark could be carried (Exodus 25:10-22; 37:1-9).

- Two cherubim figures were over the ark at each end. Their faces were turned toward each other (Exodus 37:9; Numbers 7:89), and their outstretched wings over the top formed the throne of God. The ark itself served as God's footstool (1 Chronicles 28:2).

- The ark was placed in the "Most Holy Place" (or holy of holies)—the interior portion of the tabernacle—and positioned so that one end of the carrying poles touched the veil separating the two sections of the tabernacle (1 Kings 8:8).

- Stored in the ark were the Ten Commandments on two stone tablets, the "gold jar of manna," and Aaron's "rod that budded" (Hebrews 9:4 KJV).

The Traveling Ark of the Covenant

- Before the Israelites settled in the promised land, the Kohathites would carry the ark in front of the crowds (Numbers 4:5-6).

- The book of Joshua reports that the priest carried it into the bed of the Jordan River, which separated, allowing everyone to pass through (Joshua 3:15-16).

- The ark was carried around Jericho before the Israelites took the city (Joshua 6:4-12).

- After the people of Israel settled in the promised land, the ark remained in the tabernacle of Gilgal for a while (Joshua 4:18-19). It was later moved to Shiloh (Joshua 18:1).

- The ark was sometimes carried into fields of battle in hopes of victory, but the Philistines once took the ark (1 Samuel 4:3-11). Seven months later, they returned it because it brought a curse on them (1 Samuel 5:7-8).

- After the ark was returned, it remained at Kiriath Jearim (1 Samuel 7:1-2) until the time of King David. The king wanted to move the ark to Jerusalem, but because it was not moved properly, a man named Uzzah lost his life (2 Samuel 6:3-7).

- The ark remained in the house of Obed-Edom for three months (2 Samuel 6:1-11). David then moved it to Jerusalem, where it remained until a place was prepared for it. Solomon, David's son and successor, later placed the ark in the temple he built (1 Kings 8:6-9).

- When the Babylonians sacked Jerusalem, the ark disappeared (sometime after 2 Chronicles 35:3), never to be seen again. In Revelation 11:19, however, the apostle John sees a vision of the ark.

The Life of Ezekiel

- Ezekiel was the son of a man named Buzi (Ezekiel 1:3).

- The name Ezekiel means "God strengthens."

- Ezekiel was among the people of Israel who were taken to Babylon. When he lived in Israel, he was a priest in Jerusalem.

- Ezekiel was near the Kebar River in Mesopotamia when he saw a prophetic vision of God and his cherubim (Ezekiel 1:1).

- God called Ezekiel to prophesy through a vision. God warned Ezekiel that he would be preaching to obstinate and stubborn people, but that he was not to be afraid to speak to them (Ezekiel 2:3-6).

- The number four (four living creatures, four wings, four faces) is important in the book of Ezekiel (Ezekiel 1:4-10).

- When Ezekiel's wife died, he was not allowed to grieve or mourn (Ezekiel 24:15-17).

- Like the prophet Jeremiah, Ezekiel recognized that God was using Babylon to bring judgment on his wayward people.

- After the fall of Jerusalem, the tone of Ezekiel's prophecies changes from those of doom to those of hope and encouragement.

- Ezekiel ministered from 593 to 571 BC. The Bible provides no information about him after the end of his ministry.

The Life of Hosea

- Hosea was the son of a man named Beeri.

- Hosea's name means "May the Lord save" or "deliverance."

- Hosea was probably from the nation of Israel, perhaps Samaria. He regarded Israel as his homeland.

- Hosea was married to a prostitute named Gomer and had three children: sons Jezreel and Lo-Ammi and daughter Lo-Ruhamah.

- Hosea ministered about 2750 years ago, during the reigns of the last two kings of Israel, shortly before Israel was destroyed by the Assyrian Empire (722 BC). He prophesied during the concluding years of King Jeroboam II.

- His book is the first of the 12 Minor Prophets and the longest.

- Hosea loved the nation of Israel but saw her as corrupt, evil, and wayward. His prophecies referred to the judgments that would come upon Israel because of the people's unfaithfulness to God, but they also included God's promise to restore the nation (Hosea 14:4-7).

- Hosea is well known for his terrible home life. His wife's unfaithfulness was a picture of the unfaithfulness of the nation of Israel. Just as Gomer had left home for a life of prostitution, Israel had turned away from God to pursue false gods. Despite his wife's unfaithfulness, Hosea continued to love her, pursue her, and bring her home—just as God continued to love Israel (Hosea 3:1-5).

- "Abaddon" (Revelation 9:11)

- "Accuser" (Revelation 12:10)

- "Adversary" (1 Peter 5:8 KJV)

- "Ancient serpent" (Revelation 12:9)

- "Angel of light" (2 Corinthians 11:14)

- "Angel of the Abyss" (Revelation 9:11)

- "Apollyon" (meaning Destroyer) (Revelation 9:11)

- "Beelzebub" (Matthew 12:24 KJV)

- "Belial" (2 Corinthians 6:15)

- "Deceiver" (Revelation 12:9 KJV)

- "Devil" (1 John 3:8)

- "Dragon" (Revelation 12:9)

- "Enemy" (Matthew 13:39)

- "Evil one" (Ephesians 6:16; John 17:15)

- "Father of lies" (John 8:44)

- "God of this age" (2 Corinthians 4:4)

- "Liar" (John 8:44)

- "Lucifer" (Isaiah 14:12-14 KJV)

- "Man of lawlessness" (2 Thessalonians 2:3-4)

- "Murderer" (John 8:44)

- "Prince of demons" (Luke 11:15)

- "Prince of this world" (John 12:31-32)

- "Roaring lion" (1 Peter 5:8)

- "Ruler of the kingdom of the air" (Ephesians 2:1-2)

- "Satan" (Mark 1:13)

- "Tempter" (Matthew 4:3)

- "Thief" (John 10:10)

Key Dates in the Life of Jesus

- 4 or 5 BC—His birth

- 4 or 5 BC—Journey to Egypt with his family

- 3 or 4 BC—Return from Egypt

- AD 8—Boyhood visit to the temple

- AD 26—Baptized by John the Baptist

- AD 26—First year of his ministry (Year of Inauguration)

- AD 27—Second year of his ministry (Year of Popularity)

- AD 28—Third year of his ministry (Year of Optimism)

- AD 29 or 30—Year of his death

Forty-Eight Important Titles of God

1. "Abba, Father" (Mark 14:36)

2. "Ancient of Days" (Daniel 7:9)

3. "Consuming Fire" (Hebrews 12:28-29)

4. "Creator" (Isaiah 40:28)

5. "Deliverer" (Psalm 70:5)

6. "Dwelling place" (Psalm 90:1)

7. "Eternal God" (Genesis 21:33)

8. "Father" (Isaiah 64:8)

9. "Father of our Lord Jesus Christ" (Colossians 1:3)

10. "Fortified Tower" (Proverbs 18:10)

11. "Fortress" (Jeremiah 16:19)

12. "Glorious crown" (Isaiah 28:5)

13. "God Almighty" (Genesis 17:1)

14. "God Most High" (Genesis 14:18-19)

15. "God my Savior" (Habakkuk 3:17-18)

16. "God of Abraham, Isaac, and Jacob" (Exodus 3:15)

17. "God of all comfort" (2 Corinthians 1:3)

18. "God of all the earth" (Isaiah 54:5)

19. "God of heaven" (Nehemiah 1:4)

20. "Holy One" (Isaiah 43:14-15)

21. "Horn of my salvation" (Psalm 18:2)

22. "I AM WHO I AM" (Exodus 3:14)

23. "JAH" (Psalm 68:4 KJV)

24. "Jehovah" (Exodus 6:3 KJV)

25. "Jehovah-jireh" (KJV) or "The LORD Will Provide" (Genesis 22:14)

26. "Jehovah-nissi" (KJV) or "The LORD Is My Banner" (Exodus 17:15)

27. "Jehovah-shalom" (KJV) or "The LORD Is Peace" (Judges 6:23-24)

28. "Judge" (Psalm 75:7)

29. "King" (1 Samuel 12:12)

30. "King eternal, immortal, invisible" (1 Timothy 1:17)

31. "King of glory" (Psalm 24:7-10)

32. "Lawgiver" (Isaiah 33:22)

33. "Light" (Psalm 27:1)

34. "Living God" (Daniel 6:20)

35. "LORD of hosts (Zechariah 8:22 KJV)

36. "The LORD Our Righteous Savior" (Jeremiah 23:6)

37. "The LORD, who heals" (Exodus 15:26)

38. "Majesty in heaven" (Hebrews 1:3)

39. "Potter" (Isaiah 64:8)

40. "Prince of Peace" (Isaiah 9:6)

41. "Redeemer" (Isaiah 54:8)

42. "Refuge" (Deuteronomy 33:27)

43. "Rock" (1 Samuel 2:2)

44. "Savior" (Isaiah 45:21)

45. "Shepherd" (Psalm 23:1)

46. "Shield" (Psalm 5:12)

47. "Spring of living water" (Jeremiah 2:13)

48. "Strength" (Exodus 15:2)

Twenty-Five Titles of Jesus

1. "Advocate" (1 John 2:1)

2. "Alpha and Omega" (Revelation 1:8)

3. "Anointed One" or "Messiah the Prince" (Daniel 9:25-26 KJV)

4. "Bread of life" (John 6:35)

5. "Chief Shepherd" (1 Peter 5:4)

6. "The Christ" (1 John 2:22)

7. "Faithful and true witness" (Revelation 3:14)

8. "God" (John 1:1; Hebrews 1:8; Romans 9:5)

9. "Great high priest" (Hebrews 4:14)

10. "Horn of salvation" (Luke 1:69)

11. "I am" (John 8:58)

12. "King of Kings and Lord of Lords" (Revelation 19:16)

13. "Lamb of God" (John 1:29)

14. "Last Adam" (1 Corinthians 15:45)

15. "Light of the world" (John 8:12)

16. "Lion of the tribe of Judah" (Revelation 5:5)

17. "Mediator" (1 Timothy 2:5)

18. "Mighty God" (Isaiah 9:6)

19. "Pioneer and perfecter of faith" (Hebrews 12:2)

20. "Redeemer" (Isaiah 54:5)

21. "Resurrection and the life" (John 11:25)

22. "Savior" (Ephesians 5:23; 2 Peter 2:20)

23. "Son of God" (John 1:49)

24. "Wonderful Counselor" (Isaiah 9:6)

25. "The Word" (John 1:1)

Historic Events from Christ's Birth Through the Apostle John's Death

- 37 BC–AD 4: Reign of Herod the Great, Roman-appointed king of Judea

- 4 BC–AD 6: Rule of Herod Archelaus, ethnarch of Judea, Samaria, and Idumea

- 4 BC–AD 39: Rule of Herod Antipas, tetrarch of Galilee and Perea

- 4 BC–AD 34: Rule of Herod Philip, tetrarch of Iturea and Trachonitis

- 4–6 BC: Birth of Jesus Christ

- 2 BC: Birth of Saul of Tarsus (later known as the apostle Paul)

- AD 20: Reconstruction of the temple begins

- AD 25–28: Ministry of John the Baptist

- AD 25–27: Christ's baptism

- AD 26–37: Pontius Pilate serves as prefect of Judea

- AD 29–30: Christ's crucifixion and resurrection

- AD 31–37: Conversion of Saul of Tarsus (the apostle Paul)

- AD 41: Execution of James by Herod Agrippa

- AD 45–58: Apostle Paul's missionary journeys

- AD 49: Roman Emperor Claudius expels Jews from Rome; the church holds the Council of Jerusalem

- AD 50–95: Books of the New Testament written

- AD 54: Nero becomes the Roman emperor

- AD 59–60: Paul's first imprisonment begins

- AD 62: Execution of James, the Lord's brother, in Jerusalem

- AD 67–68: Paul's final imprisonment and his death in Rome

- AD 70: Jerusalem captured by Titus; Herod's temple destroyed

- AD 81: Domitian becomes the Roman emperor

- AD 90–100: Death of the apostle John, the last living apostle

"I Am" Statements from Jesus

I am the way and the truth and the life," Jesus said (John 14:6). Here are several other "I am" statements from him:

- "I am he [the Messiah]" (John 4:25-26).

- "I am the bread of life" (John 6:35).

- "I am the living bread" (John 6:51).

- "I am from him [God]" (John 7:29).

- "I am the light of the world" (John 8:12; 9:5).

- "I am one who testifies for myself" (John 8:18).

- "I am from above" (John 8:23).

- "I am not of this world" (John 8:23).

- "Before Abraham was born, I am" (John 8:58).

- "I am the gate for the sheep" (John 10:7).

- "I am the good shepherd" (John 10:11,14).

- "I am God's Son" (John 10:36).

- "I am the resurrection and the life" (John 11:25).

- "I have come into the world as a light" (John 12:46).

- "I am in the Father, and the Father is in me" (John 14:11).

- "I am in my Father, and you are in me, and I am in you" (John 14:20).

- "I am the true vine" (John 15:1).

- "I am not of the world" (John 17:14 KJV).

- "I am the Alpha and the Omega, the First and the Last" (Revelation 22:13).

- "I am the Living One; I was dead, and now look, I am alive for ever and ever!" (Revelation 1:18).

- "I am he who searches hearts and minds" (Revelation 2:23).

- "I am the Root and the Offspring of David, and the bright Morning Star" (Revelation 22:16).

Key Miracles Performed by Jesus

- Heals Peter's mother-in-law (Matthew 8:14-15)

- Gives sight to two blind men (Matthew 9:27-31)

- Heals a man's shriveled hand (Matthew 12:9-13)

- Feeds 4000 men with a few fish and seven loaves of bread (Matthew 15:32-38)

- Walks on the water (Matthew 14:25)

- Heals man possessed by an impure spirit at Capernaum synagogue (Mark 1:23-26)

- Calms a violent storm (Mark 4:37-39)

- Heals Gadarene man who had an impure spirit (Mark 5:1-20)

- Heals Syrophoenician woman's daughter (Mark 7:24-30)

- Heals a deaf and mute man (Mark 7:31-37)

- Gives sight to a blind man of Bethsaida (Mark 8:22-26)

- Heals child possessed by a spirit (Mark 9:14-29)

- Gives sight to Bartimaeus (Mark 10:46-52)

- Arranges a miraculous catch of fish (Luke 5:4-11)

- Heals a centurion's servant (Luke 7:1-10)

- Raises a widow's son from the dead (Luke 7:11-17)

- Heals a woman "subject to bleeding" for years (Luke 8:43-48)

- Heals a man with a mute demon (Luke 11:14)

- Heals ten lepers (Luke 17:11-19)

- Turns water into wine at a wedding in Cana (John 2:1-11)

- Cures a nobleman's son in Capernaum (John 4:46-54)

- Heals a man at a pool at Bethesda (John 5:1-9)

- Gives sight to a man born blind (John 9:1-7)

- Raises Lazarus from the dead (John 11:38-44)

Places Jesus Visited

- Bethany (Matthew 26:6)
- Bethlehem (Matthew 2:1)
- Bethphage (Matthew 21:1)
- Calvary (Luke 23:33 KJV)
- Cana (John 2:11)
- Capernaum (Matthew 4:13)
- Egypt (Matthew 2:14)
- Gabbatha (John 19:13)
- Golgotha (Mark 15:22)
- Jacob's well (John 4:6)
- Jerusalem (Mark 11:11)
- Mount of Olives (John 8:1)
- Nain (Luke 7:11)
- Nazareth (Matthew 2:23)
- Peter's house (Matthew 8:14)
- Praetorium (Mark 15:16)
- Samaria (John 4:5)
- Sea of Galilee (Matthew 4:18)
- Sychar (John 4:5)
- Synagogue (Luke 4:16)
- Temple (Matthew 21:12)
- Upper room (Mark 14:15)

New Testament Examples of Putting One's Faith in Jesus

- About 3000 people in Jerusalem on the day of Pentecost (Acts 2:41)

- About 5000 men in Jerusalem (Acts 4:4)

- Unnamed multitudes of both men and women (Acts 5:14)

- Stephen (Acts 6:8)

- The Ethiopian eunuch (Acts 8:26-37)

- Aeneas (Acts 9:32-34)

- The people of Lydda and Sharon (Acts 9:35)

- The people of Joppa (Acts 9:42)

- The people of Antioch (Acts 11:20-21)

- Sergius Paulus (Acts 13:6-12)

- The lame man at Lystra (Acts 14:8-10)

- Lydia (Acts 16:14)

- The Philippian jailer and his family (Acts 16:25-31)

- Crispus and others in Corinth (Acts 18:8)

- Jews at Rome (Acts 28:17-24)

- The Ephesians (Ephesians 1:13-14)

- The Colossians (Colossians 1:2-4)

- The Thessalonians (1 Thessalonians 1:1-6)

- Eunice, Lois, and Timothy (2 Timothy 1:5)

- Philemon (Philemon 4-5)

Jesus's Seven Statements from the Cross

1. Pleading on behalf of his tormenters: "Father, forgive them, for they do not know what they are doing" (Luke 23:34).

2. Praying to God the Father: "Eli, Eli, lema sabachthani?" (which means, "My God, my God, why have you forsaken me?") (Matthew 27:46).

3. Speaking to the penitent thief on the cross: "Truly I tell you, today you will be with me in paradise" (Luke 23:43).

4. Speaking to his mother, Mary: "Woman, here is your son." Speaking to the disciple he loved: "Here is your mother." (John 19:26-27).

5. "I am thirsty" (John 19:28).

6. "Father, into your hands I commit my spirit" (Luke 23:46).

7. "It is finished" (John 19:30).

Jesus's Post-Resurrection Appearances

- To Mary Magdalene outside the empty tomb (Mark 16:9-11)

- To the other women (Matthew 28:8-10)

- To two disciples on the road to Emmaus (Luke 24:13-32)

- To the 11 remaining apostles (Luke 24:36)

- To Peter—also known as Simon or Cephas (Luke 24:34; 1 Corinthians 15:5)

- To the apostles, except for Thomas (John 20:19-25)

- To the 11 apostles (John 20:26-31)

- To seven apostles at the Sea of Galilee (John 21:1-23)

- To 500 believers, male and female (1 Corinthians 15:6)

- To James and then to all the apostles (1 Corinthians 15:7)

- To the disciples present at the time of his ascension (Luke 24:36-50)

- To Paul at his conversion (Acts 9:1-19; 1 Corinthians 15:8)

What Does It Mean That Jesus Ascended into Heaven?

After he said this, he was taken up before their very eyes, and a cloud hid him from their sight. They were looking intently up into the sky as he was going, when suddenly two men dressed in white stood beside them. "Men of Galilee," they said, "why do you stand here looking into the sky? This same Jesus, who has been taken from you into heaven, will come back in the same way you have seen him go into heaven."

ACTS 1:9-11

O ver the years, more than one skeptic has questioned the notion that Jesus ascended into heaven before the very eyes of his disciples. In this view, even if Jesus were traveling at the speed of light, he would not yet have escaped the confines of our universe. Not only that, but the lack of oxygen would have surely been a problem.

Jesus's ascending into heaven does not, however, imply that he traveled through physical space. Rather, this God-man *transcended* time and space. Put another way, heaven is not located in time and space; it exists in another dimension.

Furthermore, the physical universe does not exhaust reality. It doesn't take a rocket scientist to understand that an effect such as the universe must have a cause greater than itself.

This is self-evident not only to those who are philosophically sophisticated but also to thoughtful people everywhere. So the notion that the Creator of the universe transcended his own universe should pose no problem.

Finally, God often uses physical examples to point to spiritual realities; thus, the physical fact of Christ's ascension points to the greater truth that he is now glorified in the presence of God and that our glorification is divinely guaranteed as well.

What Does It Mean When the Holy Spirit Is Within You?

Do you not know that your bodies are temples of the Holy Spirit, who is in you, whom you have received from God?

1 CORINTHIANS 6:19

What do we really mean when we say, "God is in my heart; the Holy Spirit is in me"? Does this mean everyone simultaneously has a little piece of God inside? Or is the Bible communicating a truth far more precious?

First, to say that the Holy Spirit is *in* you is not to point out *where* the Holy Spirit is physically, but rather to acknowledge that you have come into an intimate, personal relationship with him through faith and repentance. As such, the preposition *in* is not a *locational* but a *relational* term. Similarly, when Jesus says, "The Father is in me, and I in the Father" (John 10:38), he is not speaking of physical location but of the intimacy of a relationship.

Furthermore, to deny that the Holy Spirit is *spatially* locatable within us is not to deny that he is actively locatable within us, working redemptively to conform us to the image of Christ. Far from detracting from our nearness to the Holy Spirit, the classic Christian view intensifies the intimacy of our relationship to the Creator as well as the benefits of our redemption.

According to the Scriptures, the Holy Spirit is not a physical being. To ask, "Where is the Holy Spirit?" merely invites confusion. Asking spatial questions about a being who does not have extension in space makes about as much sense as asking what the color blue tastes like.

King Solomon reveals the utter futility of trying to physically locate the spiritual when he asks, "Will God really dwell on earth? The heavens, even the highest heaven, cannot contain you. How much less this temple I have built!" (1 Kings 8:27).

PART 2

Things We Say
from the Bible

Adam's Apple

W hile the term *Adam's apple* has nothing to do with the Scriptures, its origin does link to the first man, who was named Adam.

In the mid-1700s, English law forbade surgeons to dissect the human body—with the exception of executed murderers. As a result, cadavers were hard to come by. Thanks to William Hunter, a medical visionary, dissection was introduced to the medical community circa 1747 as he and his students tackled identifying and naming the internal body parts of humans.

Scientists were grateful; the public was outraged.

Politics aside, however, it was one innocent, little probe into the male neck that posed the greatest of all challenges. A lump there kept moving, dodging the surgeon's scalpel and darting about under the skin, even though the subject of the dissection was quite lifeless.

As legend had long held that the Adam's apple was a piece of the *forbidden fruit* that got stuck in Adam's throat when he committed that early sin, Hunter and his colleagues let the lump slide (literally). In an effort to blend science with the biblical story *and folklore*, they named this troublesome lump the Adam's apple.

Wouldn't Know Him from Adam

The common phrase "Wouldn't know him from Adam" isn't scriptural. It's a reference to a person we simply do not know.

Given that Adam was created, not born attached to an umbilical cord, some have contemplated that no navel would have existed. So technically, we could pick Adam out of a lineup, provided he was wearing no more than a fig leaf. But arguing this point doesn't lend insight to the expression's meaning.

To give credit where credit is due, the phrase in its entirety is "Don't know him from Adam's off ox," made popular in the mid-1800s via a book of Nantucket colloquialisms. "Wouldn't know him from Adam's house cat" is a variation of the same expression.

Regardless of the animal you might have tacked onto the end of this phrase, "Wouldn't know him from Adam" is just another way of saying "Couldn't pick him out of a crowd of two."

Be Fruitful and Multiply

The command to "be fruitful, and multiply" (KJV) means exactly what you think it does: Go populate the earth. The phrase is spoken no fewer than six times in the book of Genesis alone, making procreation Adam and Eve's number one job at the opening of the story (Genesis 1:28). Makes sense, as someone had to get the human race going.

The next reference is in Genesis 9:1. Here, God exhorts Noah and his sons to "be fruitful, and multiply" (Genesis 9:28-29 KJV). Noah himself may or may not have been much help at this stage, given that he was 600 years old when he came off the ark. But it's safe to assume that the brunt of this burden fell upon his three sons: Ham, Shem, and Japheth.

Curse of Eve

While the earliest curse is scriptural, it wasn't directed to Eve, but rather to the serpent who tempted her. Genesis 3:16 is a litany of punishment God bestows upon Eve for eating from the tree she was told to avoid. Technically, however, the curse was placed on the serpent that tempted Eve.

From the Hebrew word *etsab*, Eve's punishment is "labor"—both childbirth labor and physical labor—along with punishment and consequences for Adam. Curiously, the King James Version translates the same word as "sorrow." The question becomes, Was Eve's pain physical or was it emotional? It was both. Some suggest Eve's curse goes beyond the physical pain of childbirth and extends to the emotional pain a mother would feel for her children's future.

At a minimum, this would be a postpartum depression of exponential proportion, considering that Eve, now banned from her perfect home, would carry the burden of what her actions cost her children. Eve's curse would extend beyond raw physical pain to knowing her family would never experience the perfect world she once enjoyed, thanks to her choices.

Pain. Sorrow. The punishment is real. Eve now must work to survive. Life outside of Eden would be no picnic. We only need to factor in the birth pain element alone to know that this curse was going to change life for Eve and for every future generation.

Sweat of Your Brow

GENESIS 3:19

A reference to work, the "sweat of your brow" in Genesis 3:19 is anything that connotes physical labor. Specifically, the expression from the King James Version states:

> In the sweat of thy face shalt thou eat bread, till thou return unto the ground; for out of it wast thou taken: for dust thou art, and unto dust shalt thou return.

By way of Adam and Eve's story, work becomes punishment for disobedience. They must now factor in the day-to-day activities required for their survival.

Was work a paradise before? This question remains unanswered. However, we know Adam already had tasks to do. He was put in the garden to "work it and take care of it" (Genesis 2:15). But this we also know: Once Adam and Eve sinned, life changed dramatically for them. Their routines of walking and talking with God were now replaced by physical labor and physical pain.

Not only would they struggle by the sweat of their brow, but they would likewise be destined to return to the dust from which they were created, which suggests life became a lot more stressful than originally intended.

The Fall of Man

The concept of the expression "the fall of man" is doctrinal. However, while the concept traces to Genesis, the actual words are not found in Scripture. Rather, the phrase is one of theological creation, summing up the scene after Adam and Eve are cast out of the Garden of Eden.

As the couple fell from their original state of purity and innocence, their disobedience caused humankind to suffer in sin (that is, until Jesus died and covered the sins of those who believe in him as their personal Lord and Savior).

The immediate ramifications continue today: Serpents have to belly-crawl, women experience great pain in childbirth, and men will forever struggle to grow crops from land that was once fertile. But the greatest tragedy of the fall is that it introduces the spiritual separation of creation (humankind) from the Creator (God).

Beyond these specifics, the fall is the result of poor choices made by our first human ambassadors—those who could not resist taking the forbidden fruit from the tree of the knowledge of good and evil.

Ashes to Ashes...Dust to Dust

In Genesis 3:19, after Adam and Eve sinned, God told them, "Dust you are and to dust you will return."

The dust part we have figured out. As humans, we are made of earthly elements. But when called on the carpet after breaking God's commandment, Adam and Eve quickly got the first glimpse of their future when God talked about dust.

"Dust to dust" in this context refers to humanity's mortality—the ultimate punishment for lives now filled with human struggles and pain. First hard work, then agonizing pain, and, ultimately, death are the consequences of disobedience.

"Ashes to ashes" is not scriptural. It comes from the *Book of Common Prayer*, added for recitation at Anglican burial services. To be precise, the phrase most commonly referenced is "Earth to earth, ashes to ashes...dust to dust; in sure and certain hope of the Resurrection to eternal life."

Raising Cain

A modern colloquialism stemming from the biblical story of Cain, "raising Cain" suggests a ruckus or a great disturbance.

"Raising Cain," of course, springs from the Genesis 4 account of Cain (son of Adam and Eve), whose vegetarian offering was rejected by God in favor of his brother's animal sacrifice. The plot thickened when jealousy overtook Cain and he killed that brother, Abel.

As punishment, God curses the ground that Cain, as a farmer, would work. He curses Cain as well, exiling him to a life of wandering.

The phrase "raising Cain" is not found in the Bible. It first appeared in an 1840s comic strip in the *St. Louis Pennant*. This usage referred to trouble-making, rather than poor childrearing, and that same connotation prevails today.

Am I My Brother's Keeper?

GENESIS 4:9-16

The line "Am I my brother's keeper?" belongs to Cain, firstborn of Adam and Eve, the Bible's first recorded murderer. The plot is this: Cain kills Abel out of jealousy. God comes knocking and asks, "Where is your brother Abel?"

Cain replies, "I don't know." Cain is lying, of course. He makes matters worse when he asks, "Am I my brother's keeper?"

From here, curses abound. Cain is cursed. The ground from which Cain derived his livelihood is cursed, which for a farmer is a double curse. The Bible goes on to tell us, "Cain went out from the LORD's presence and lived in the land of Nod, east of Eden."

Meanwhile, though cursed, Cain is still God's own. He is protected from harm by way of a mark (Genesis 4:15), which provides *another* classic phrase, "the mark of Cain."

As Old as Methuselah

GENESIS 5:27

Methuselah was Noah's great-great-grandpa, and many believe he's the oldest man in recorded history. The Genesis account tells us Methuselah lived to be 969 years old. (More impressive than his longevity, he was still fathering sons when he was 187 years old.) Methuselah has become the proverbial symbol of longevity.

The expression "as old as Methuselah" stretches back as far as the fourteenth century, which makes the phrase almost as old as the man was himself. Ironically, when compared to other ancient Near Eastern writings that reference the antediluvian (preflood) kings, others lived for thousands of years. This means that, at least by some standards of record keeping, Methuselah was not the oldest person in history.

We have no way to know how years were counted back then, but given that Genesis goes to great length to factor the ages into Noah's genealogy, it's interesting to attempt the math. Apparently, Methuselah would have still been alive as Noah was boarding the animals onto the ark. Sadly, he died the same year the flooding began.

Promised Land

Also known as Canaan, Canaan's Land, and the Land of Milk and Honey, the promised land was territory God promised to Abraham, Isaac, and Jacob on behalf of the children of Israel.

To Abraham, God promised:

> To your descendants I give this land, from the Wadi of Egypt to the great river, the Euphrates (Genesis 15:18).

To Abraham's son Isaac, God promised:

> To you and your descendants I will give all these lands (Genesis 26:3).

To Isaac's son Jacob, God promised:

> I will give you and your descendants the land on which you are lying (Genesis 28:13).

When God freed the children of Israel from slavery in Egypt, he planned for their leader, Moses, to escort them into the promised land. The Israelites eventually did reach it, but Moses did not. He failed to trust God's instruction to merely speak into a rock to bring forth water, instead striking the rock with a rod (Numbers 20:1-12). God was not pleased.

Deuteronomy 34:1 tells us Moses later "climbed Mount Nebo from the plains of Moab to the top of Pisgah, across from Jericho. There the Lord showed him the whole land" from Gilead to Zoar. As Moses looked out on the promised land, God told him, "I have let you see it with your eyes, but you will not cross over into it" (verse 4).

Civil rights activist Martin Luther King Jr. made perhaps the most well-known reference to both the promised land and Moses's time on the mountain. In his famous speech commonly called "I've Been to the Mountaintop," Dr. King aligned his vision with Moses's experience, saying God had allowed him, too, to "go up to the mountain."

"I've seen the promised land," he said. "I may not get there with you. But I want you to know tonight, that we, as a people, will get to the promised land."

In this speech, the promised land is forever metaphorical, symbolizing a time when all people will someday live together as complete equals, regardless of race. Today others might define the promised land as simply a better place and say they've been to the mountaintop because they have seen—or envisioned—that better place.

Jacob's Ladder

GENESIS 28:13-17

W hile sleeping on a pillow made of stone, Jacob had a now-famous dream featuring a ladder reaching into heaven. With angels ascending and angels descending, he hears the voice of God say:

> I am the LORD, the God of your father Abraham and the God of Isaac. I will give you and your descendants the land on which you are lying...All peoples on earth will be blessed through you and your offspring" (Genesis 28:13-14).

Upon waking, Jacob concludes he has literally been in the presence of God. In awestruck fear, he declares this place to be "the gate of heaven" (Genesis 28:17).

Years later, a pillar is anointed and named Bethel—memorializing the place where Jacob first vows to make the Lord his God. Keep in mind that Jacob will soon receive a new name: *Israel*. But when people think of that famous ladder, they think *Jacob*.

Land o' Goshen

GENESIS 45:10

In Southern vernacular, *Land o' Goshen* is right up there with *Heavens to Betsy*. But unlike Betsy's heaven, Goshen was a real place. Located in the northeast part of the Nile Delta, Goshen boasted green pastures—lush and particularly desirable grazing lands for sheep and cattle.

This same land was offered by Joseph, who was now rubbing elbows with Pharaoh, as a new home for his brothers and his father. This is two years into Egypt's seven-year famine—a famine predicted in Pharaoh's dream about the fat and skinny cows.

In short, Goshen was some of Egypt's finest turf. Specifically, we're told:

> You shall live in the region of Goshen and be near me—
> you, your children and grandchildren, your flocks and
> herds, and all you have (Genesis 45:10).

The reference comes after Joseph was sold by his jealous brothers into slavery. When a turn of events puts Joseph in charge just as his brothers come in search of food, they discover that their brother is alive, well, and quite powerful.

With five more years of famine still on the horizon, Joseph implores his brothers to bring their father (Jacob) and move with him and their families to the land of Goshen, a windfall of a gift in light of the cruel manner in which they had treated him earlier.

Today the expression is much akin to "For goodness' sake!" and signifying a pleasant outcome, coming from the last place (or person) you would expect.

An Eye for an Eye…a Tooth for a Tooth

The concept of "an eye for an eye" is a biblical legal term and quite simple in meaning. Today we might call it "tit for tat."

Under Mosaic law, anyone who took the eye of another, whether intentionally or by accident, would face equal retribution. Scholars believe it was designed to keep the level of punishment to a minimum, allowing retribution to equal only that of the precise crime, and no more.

This principle is noted throughout the Old Testament. However, Jesus overturned this notion in his Sermon on the Mount, where he added a new, more compassionate addendum:

> You have heard that it was said, "Eye for eye, and tooth for tooth." But I tell you, do not resist an evil person. If anyone slaps you on the right cheek, turn to them the other cheek also (Matthew 5:38-39).

Keep in mind, the principle applied to more than just eyes and teeth. In its original form, any body part could be substituted (a hand for a hand, a foot for a foot).

While most scholars credit Moses as the originator of the concept, some credit the Code of Hammurabi (one of the earliest sets of laws known to man), which can be traced back to ancient Babylon (circa 1760 BC), hundreds of years before the time of Moses.

Apple of My Eye

DEUTERONOMY 32:10

Have you ever wondered, *What is with the apple, and whose eye are we talking about?* This phrase references someone held dear. The object of this great affection would (by definition) be someone's pride and joy. In scriptural context, this object is God's children, Israel.

The eye? That would be God's eye, ever watching over his own. The Song of Moses states:

> In a desert land he found him, in a barren and howling waste. He shielded him and cared for him; he guarded him as the apple of his eye (Deuteronomy 32:10).

A metaphor referenced no fewer than five times as the nation of Israel evolves, it's no wonder we all know this expression. Repetition alone suggests that when it comes to the children of Israel, they are considered special. Their Father (God) loves them so much.

Let's look at some other examples. In the book of Psalms, David appeals to God, requesting:

> Keep me as the apple of your eye; hide me in the shadow of your wings (Psalm 17:8).

In Proverbs 7:2, Solomon says, "Keep my commands and you will live; guard my teachings as the apple of your eye."

Two other references to this favored status are in Lamentations (2:18) and Zechariah (2:8), but the bottom line is this: There are many apples, but God's children are the originals.

Hit the Nail on the Head

JUDGES 4:17-21

Some people trace this expression to merchants who nailed bogus money to their shop doors as fair warning to anyone who might consider the notion of counterfeiting. Most people understand it to mean someone has landed on what's entirely accurate.

To be fair, this phrase is not found verbatim in Scripture, but the expression takes on biblical significance because of one of the best (and most gruesome) stories to come out of the Old Testament. In the book of Judges, we find a woman named Jael, who made the expression literal.

The story, about an assassination predicted by the judge and prophetess Deborah, is a rather bloody one. When Sisera, an enemy of Israel, flees the battlefield and seeks shelter from God's chosen, he thinks he's found comfort in the tent of Jael, a supposed ally. We are told Jael took Sisera into her tent, gave him milk, and covered him with a blanket. But as he slept, the Bible reveals, Jael, wife of Heber, approached and "went quietly to him while he lay fast asleep, exhausted. She drove the peg through his temple into the ground, and he died" (Judges 4:21).

This was a rather gruesome ending, but it did net Israel many years of peace—40 years, to hit the nail on the head.

As Old as the Hills

JOB 15:7

Some might toss the phrase "as old as the hills" right in there with such classics as "older than God's dog." However, that is a mistake. God's dog, assuming he even has one, is not mentioned in the Bible. "As old as the hills," on the other hand, is both traceable and scriptural.

The expression can be traced back to Job, who has gone through a series of hard—even tragic—knocks. In processing his plight with friends, Job ponders the nature of God, debating whether God's relationship to humankind is one of benevolent intercessor or indifferent creator.

In a series of philosophical questions that would make Socrates proud, Job offers a number of theological theories as he struggles to make sense of his underserved suffering—the scriptural equivalent of "Why do bad things happen to good people?"

The idea that someone could be "as old as the hills" is first implied by Job's friend Eliphaz in his effort to convince Job that his suffering is not without meaning. Eliphaz suggests that God's wisdom is greater than Job's comprehension when he poses this rhetorical query: "Are you the first man ever born? Were you brought forth before the hills?" (Job 15:7).

By the Skin of My Teeth

Job 19:20

O bviously, teeth don't have skin, although some scholars suggest "by the skin of my teeth" could refer to that thin, porcelain like layer of tooth enamel.

Unlike some modern-day translations, the King James Version tells us Job says not "by the skin of my teeth," but "with the skin of my teeth": "My bone cleaveth to my skin and to my flesh, and I am escaped with the skin of my teeth" (Job 19:20). This suggests that after all Job's trials, especially his physical trials, he has come out on the other side with very little left.

Regardless, the colorful expression today speaks to a narrow escape. The phrase was popularized by American humorist Thornton Wilder.

Out of the Mouth of Babes

PSALM 8:2

Although it is straight from the Bible, the familiar expression "out of the mouth of babes" (KJV) is often credited to Shakespeare. But Jesus made it noteworthy when he referenced an Old Testament psalm while speaking to the chief priests and scribes (Matthew 21:15-17).

Modern interpretations range from "kids say the darndest things" to the godlike wisdom found in innocence. But to truly understand the phrase, it helps to review what Psalm 8:1-2 (KJV) states:

> O LORD, our Lord, how excellent is thy name in all the earth! who hast set thy glory above the heavens. Out of the mouth of babes and sucklings hast thou ordained strength because of thine enemies, that thou mightest still the enemy and the avenger.

In this song of praise, the psalmist uses "out of the mouth of babes" to express God's ability to employ his might via unlikely sources.

Jesus's reference to the same concept, spoken just as the masses are singing his praises, is timely, if not a little cryptic. Having just rebuked the moneychangers in the temple for turning his "house of prayer" into a "den of thieves" (Matthew 21:13 KJV), Jesus's choice of passage is rich in its implications:

> Yea; have ye never read, Out of the mouth of babes and sucklings thou hast perfected praise? (Matthew 21:16 KJV).

With children singing "Hosanna" to the son of David, the scene, like the psalm Jesus references, speaks of truth uttered from innocence, a song of praise coming "out of the mouth of babes."

At Their Wit's End

PSALM 107:27

A t their wit's end" is an expression as popular today as when it was first penned. People at their wit's end are frazzled. They're eaten up with worry or exasperation, most likely from repeated attempts to resolve a matter all by themselves.

What most people don't know is that the first mention of anyone being at this *wit's end* appears in the Bible in the book of Psalms. Listing a litany of stressful scenarios, the expression in its entirety reads:

> They reel to and fro, and stagger like a drunken man, and are at their wit's end (Psalm 107:27 KJV).

These words appear in a prayer of thanksgiving, as the psalmist describes the fear of a storm-tossed sailor, miraculously saved by calling on the Lord. In biblical, colorful commentary, the writer depicts a seasick scenario, complete with the panic that would naturally ensue. Interestingly, the Hebrew word for *wit* is more akin to *wisdom*, suggesting that people at the end of their wit have lost their ability to reason, to solve a problem wisely.

Some call the verse prophetic—an Old Testament foreshadowing of one of Jesus's experiences in the New Testament—involving a boat, his disciples, and a storm. The rocking and reeling are reminiscent of the Old Testament passage. However, this story ends with three simple words: "Peace, be still" (Mark 4:39 KJV). With these words, Jesus calmed the raging sea, so no one on his boat wound up at his *wit's end*.

Spare the Rod...Spoil the Child

While the book of Proverbs provides ample words of wisdom frequently quoted today, "spare the rod and spoil the child" is nowhere to be found in Proverbs or anywhere else in Scripture.

True, several references to corporal punishment are in the book of Proverbs, but the precise wording of Proverbs 13:24 is:

> Whoever spares the rod hates their children, but the one who loves their children is careful to discipline them.

In Proverbs 22:15, we also find:

> Folly is bound up in the heart of a child, but the rod of discipline will drive it far away.

And in Proverbs 23:14, we find the more graphic citation:

> Punish him with the rod and save his soul from death.

To give credit where credit is due, the poetic, more commonly cited expression was the creation of Samuel Butler in his satiric poem "Hudibras" (1664). Butler writes:

> Love is a boy by poets styled; then spare the rod and spoil the child.

Of course, another side to the rod departs from the world of discipline and punishment. Indeed, let us not forget that rod and staff are symbols of *comfort* in the often-cited Twenty-Third Psalm. Verse 4 reads:

> Your rod and your staff, they comfort me.

To Everything There Is a Season

ECCLESIASTES 3:1-8

Who knew we were memorizing Scripture when we were singing the Pete Seeger–penned hit "Turn, Turn, Turn"? (Seeger wrote the song in the late 1950s, but it didn't become an international hit until the Byrds recorded it in 1965.)

The original "lyrics" were ecclesiastical—meaning having to do with church or clergy. They appear in the Old Testament book of Ecclesiastes, written in the persona of Solomon. These timeless words are still admired today as some of the purest poetry ever written.

While open to interpretation, the essence of the tune is one of perspective, placing the elements of life into cycles best viewed not as right or wrong, but more as the natural and inevitable ebb and flow of life. In its entirety, the familiar Scripture reads:

> To every thing there is a season, and a time to every purpose under the heaven:
> A time to be born, and a time to die; a time to plant, and a time to pluck up that which is planted;
> A time to kill, and a time to heal; a time to break down, and time to build up;
> A time to weep, and a time to laugh; a time to mourn, and a time to dance;
> A time to cast away stones, and a time to gather stones together; a time to embrace, and a time to refrain from embracing;
> A time to get, and a time to lose; a time to keep, and a time to cast away;
> A time to rend, and a time to sew; a time to keep silence, and time to speak;
> A time to love, and a time to hate; a time of war, and time of peace (KJV).

A Drop in a Bucket

ISAIAH 40:15

The "a drop in a bucket" expression is the epitome of "the big picture is what's important." The original passage was spoken by a prophet living in exile who prophesied to the children of Israel and assured them their Babylonian captivity would soon come to an end. The passage was another way of saying that, in the larger context, their enemy's oppression would be but a blip on the radar.

> Surely the nations are like a drop in a bucket; they are regarded as dust on the scales (Isaiah 40:15).

So common is the phrase that people often forget it is scriptural. In fact, these words have been mistakenly credited to various sources, including the *Edinburgh Weekly Journal*. But the original expression was coined by Isaiah, as he reminded the faithful that neither nature nor nations would deter the plan of God.

No Rest for the Weary

ISAIAH 57:20-21

"No rest for the weary" suggests one must keep on keeping on, no matter how tired or overworked.

A similar phrase appears even earlier, in Old Testament literature: "no peace for the wicked." This variation bears a slightly edgier connotation. The implication is that the devil never sleeps, nor does he allow his followers to rest from their plotting and planning. While this phrase has appeared periodically over the centuries, the original hails from the book of Isaiah:

> The wicked are like the tossing sea, which cannot rest, whose waves cast up mire and mud. "There is no peace," says my God, "for the wicked" (Isaiah 57:20-21).

It's possible that the "weary" version of the saying also comes from the Bible. In Lamentations 5:5, most likely written more than 100 years after the Isaiah passages, we read, "Those who pursue us are at our heels; we are weary and find no rest."

Sour Grapes

The mere mention of *sour grapes* takes most of us back to Aesop's fable titled "The Fox and the Grapes." A fox, struggling to reach grapes high on a vine, eventually gives up, rationalizing, "Those grapes were sour anyway."

The fable's moral: It's easy to find fault with goals you can't attain. But the phrase turns scriptural when the prophet Ezekiel asks God to explain a proverb involving the same concept. We read:

> What do you people mean by quoting this proverb about the land of Israel: "The parents eat sour grapes, and the children's teeth are set on edge"? (Ezekiel 18:2).

Now, we don't know whether Ezekiel is referencing the tale handed down from the time of Aesop (a slave and storyteller in ancient Greece from 620–560 BC), but we do know that certain expressions repeated over time as they are conveyed from culture to culture take on new meaning. In Aesop's fable, *sour grapes* refers to someone rationalizing failure when the goal is not attained. In Ezekiel's book, *sour grapes* speaks to a question of personal responsibility.

In response, God assures Ezekiel that each individual will be judged by his or her own actions, that the sins of the father will not be held against future generations.

Incidentally, the word *fable* comes from the Latin *fabula*, which means "story." On a similar note, *proverb* derives from the Latin *proverbium*, meaning "a story with a moral or lesson." Both were key literary devices used to illustrate a point.

The Salt of the Earth

MATTHEW 5:13; LUKE 14:34

An expression that traces straight to the Sermon on the Mount, "the salt of the earth" refers to a person who's decent, solid, and dependable. The specific reference Jesus made is in both Matthew and Luke.

A universal preservative, salt was an absolute necessity in Jesus's day. The element was known for its life-sustaining qualities. The Roman word *salarium* (source of our word *salary*) sprang from the fact that Roman soldiers were often paid in salt—valued for its preservative qualities, especially in those days prior to refrigeration.

But this is only half the story. Various Old Testament references for salt abound.

Leviticus 2:13 instructs that offerings should be seasoned with salt.

Ezekiel 16:4 describes how infants were rubbed with (finely ground) salt for good health.

From the land of the Dead Sea, salt was not only purifying; it was life preserving—a stable, solid compound that was highly valued.

As salt retains these qualities even today, some suggest Jesus's reference to salt of the earth was an admonishment to his followers to season and preserve the world by participating in and reaching out to the world around them, as opposed to removing themselves from it.

MATTHEW 6:3

Contrasting and comparing the motives between hypocrites (from the Greek word *hypokrisis*, meaning "playacting") and those driven by selfless motives, the Gospel of Matthew speaks repeatedly against those whose intentions are not pure.

The reference to the left hand not knowing what the right hand is doing alludes to giving for the virtue of giving alone and not for credit or praise. The expression means, simply, "Give and get on with it!"

The Scripture in its entirety reads:

> When you give to the needy, do not let your left hand know what your right hand is doing.

In business, the phrase is often equated with keeping one's various enterprises separate. In government, the expression carries a more negative connotation, suggesting a lack of shared knowledge. But in scriptural context, the expression is pure and simple: Selfless giving requires no audience.

Wolf in Sheep's Clothing

MATTHEW 7:15

A metaphor for an enemy who pretends to be your friend, "a wolf in sheep's clothing" is another classic from the Sermon on the Mount. But the Aesop fable titled "The Wolf in Sheep's Clothing," dating back to the sixth century BC, provides the first example of this famous expression.

The story centers on a hungry wolf that discovers a sheep's fleece on the ground. By draping himself in it, the wolf finds a covert way to get closer to his prey—some unsuspecting sheep!

In scriptural context, a similar image is depicted in Matthew 7:15:

> Watch out for false prophets. They come to you in sheep's clothing, but inwardly they are ferocious wolves.

Because wandering prophets with varying messages were commonplace in the towns and villages of Jesus's day, the meaning of the admonition was quite simple: "Beware the messenger."

But to help you know your sheep from your wolves, Jesus offers the ultimate test for spotting false prophets. In the next verse he notes:

> By their fruit you will recognize them (Matthew 7:16).

The Blind Leading the Blind

MATTHEW 15:14

An expression you hear quite often in everyday conversation, "the blind leading the blind" depicts an all-too-common scenario. The phrase is credited to Jesus in Matthew's Gospel. That Scripture reads:

> Leave them; they are blind guides. If the blind lead the blind, both will fall into a pit (Matthew 15:14).

However, to give credit where credit is due, this concept predates Matthew's account. It can be tracked back as far as the seventh century BC. In some early Hindu texts, we find a similar reference.

From the Katha Upanishad:

> Abiding in the midst of ignorance, thinking themselves wise and learned, fools go aimlessly higher and thither, like blind led by the blind.

Is anything more frustrating than watching an uninformed person trying to instruct others who are equally ignorant?

Burning the Midnight Oil

MATTHEW 25:6-10

Not to be confused with burning the candle at both ends, "burning the midnight oil" refers to someone who toils deep into the night. But scripturally the meaning goes much deeper, having to do with being ever ready for the return of the Messiah.

However, the exact wording is nowhere in the Bible.

In the parable of the ten virgins, Jesus likens the kingdom of heaven to ten virgins: five wise, five foolish. The latter took no oil for their lamps, while the wise were always prepared.

In Matthew 25:6-10 we read

> At midnight the cry rang out: "Here's the bridegroom! Come out to meet him!" Then all the virgins woke up and trimmed their lamps. The foolish ones said to the wise, "Give us some of your oil; our lamps are going out." "No," they replied, "there may not be enough for both us and you. Instead, go to those who sell oil and buy some for yourselves." But while they were on their way to buy the oil, the bridegroom arrived. The virgins who were ready went in with him to the wedding banquet. And the door was shut.

A passage synonymous with eternal preparation, the story is a reminder to be in a perpetual state of readiness for the Lord's return.

O Ye of Little Faith

MATTHEW/LUKE

Spoken in a religious context, "O ye of little faith" is a rebuke to anyone who lacks faith. Spoken in a secular context, the expression has become a humorous response to one whose beliefs, if not abilities, are in question. Either way, the biblical chiding appears several times and is always spoken by Jesus to those near him, to people who never quite grasp the true power of his divinity. A classic example is Matthew's account of Jesus's calming of the storm—and his panicked disciples:

> His disciples came to him, and awoke him, saying, Lord, save us: we perish. And he saith unto them, Why are ye fearful, O ye of little faith? Then he arose, and rebuked the winds and the sea; and there was a great calm (Matthew 8:25-26 KJV).

Consider, too, Peter's attempt to walk on water—when he momentarily lapses into disbelief. Scripture states:

> When he saw the wind boisterous, he was afraid; and beginning to sink he cried, saying, Lord, save me. And immediately Jesus stretched forth his hand, and caught him, and said unto him, O thou of little faith, wherefore didst thou doubt? (Matthew 14:30-31 KJV).

Then there is Luke's account, where Jesus says:

> Consider the lilies how they grow; they toil not, they spin not; and yet I say unto you, that Solomon in all his glory was not arrayed like one of these. If then God so clothe the grass, which is to day in the field, and tomorrow is cast into the oven; how much more will he clothe you, O ye of little faith? (Luke 12:27-28 KJV).

Baptism by Fire

Often credited to a French source referring to the first fire of the battlefield, the original "baptism by fire" took place in the days following Jesus's resurrection. Acts 2:3-4 describes the scene:

> They saw what seemed to be tongues of fire that separated and came to rest on each of them. All of them were filled with the Holy Spirit and began to speak in other tongues as the Spirit enabled them.

From the Greek *baptisma pyros*, this fire baptism became the symbol for martyrs throughout antiquity.

For Christians, it has come to represent the baptism of the Holy Spirit, foretold by John the Baptist in Matthew 3:11 and in Luke 3:16.

For everyone else, the expression means your mettle has been tested—a pun of sorts, considering that fire is how we test and purify metals on earth.

PART 3

Bible Knowledge
Challenge

General Bible Questions

1. How many books are in the Bible?

    a. 47

    b. 55

    c. 66

    d. 70

2. How many books are in the Old Testament?

    a. 37

    b. 39

    c. 41

    d. 43

3. How many books are in the New Testament?

    a. 24

    b. 25

    c. 26

    d. 27

4. What is the shortest book of the Bible?

    a. Obadiah

    b. Malachi

    c. Philemon

    d. 3 John

5. What is the longest book in the Bible?

    a. Jeremiah

    b. Psalms

    c. Isaiah

    d. Genesis

6. What is the shortest book in the Old Testament?

    a. Ruth

    b. Obadiah

    c. Haggai

    d. Zephaniah

7. What is the longest book of the New Testament?

    a. Luke

    b. Acts

    c. Matthew

    d. Revelation

8. How many chapters are in the entire Bible?

    a. 587

    b. 898

    c. 1,189

    d. 1,667

9. Which of the following books contains the Ten Commandments?

    a. Genesis

b. Leviticus

c. Deuteronomy

d. Numbers

10. Which three books are referred to as the Major Prophets?

a. Isaiah, Jeremiah, and Ezekiel

b. Isaiah, Daniel, and Jonah

c. Jeremiah, Hosea, and Malachi

d. Jeremiah, Daniel, and Nehemiah

11. Which Old Testament book(s) do/does not mention God?

a. Ruth

b. Esther

c. Song of Solomon (or Song of Songs)

d. Zephaniah

e. Both b and c

12. Which is the correct order of the New Testament Gospels?

a. Mark, Matthew, Luke, John

b. Matthew, Mark, Luke, John

c. Matthew, Mark, John, Luke

d. Mark, Matthew, John, Luke

13. How many letters of the New Testament did the apostle Paul write?

a. 9

b. 11

c. 13

d. 16

14. Which Gospel contains Jesus's Sermon on the Mount?

a. Matthew

b. Mark

c. Luke

d. John

15. Which Old Testament book prophesied that Jesus would be born in Bethlehem?

a. Malachi

b. Daniel

c. Isaiah

d. Micah

16. The Bible is the world's most translated book.

a. True

b. False

17. The wisdom books of the Bible are Job, Psalms, Proverbs, Ecclesiastes, and Song of Solomon (or Song of Songs).

a. True

b. False

18. Acts is the book that covers the history of the early church.

a. True

b. False

19. Jude and Philemon are the apocalyptic books of the Bible.

    a. True

    b. False

20. How many times does the name "God" appear in the King James Version of the Bible?

    a. 2,908

    b. 3,358

    c. 4,473

    d. 7,193

Old Testament Questions

1. Eve was created from which part of Adam's body?

    a. heart

    b. leg

    c. rib

    d. brain

2. In what order did God create the elements of the universe?

    a. the heavens and the earth; day and night; land and vegetation; fish and birds; sun, moon, and stars; land animals

    b. day and night; sun, moon, and stars; sky and sea; fish and birds; land and vegetation; land animals

    c. sky and sea; day and night; sun, moon, and stars; land and vegetation; fish and birds; land animals

    d. day and night; sky and sea; land and vegetation; sun, moon, and stars; birds and fish; land animals

3. God commanded Adam and Eve to eat only from the tree of the knowledge of good and evil in the garden of Eden.

    a. True

    b. False

4. What classic phrase begins the serpent's speech to Eve in his scheme to get her to sin?

    a. "Thou shalt not covet......"

    b. "Do you want to be like God…"

c. "Did God really say…"

d. "All these I will give you…"

5. What did Adam and Eve sew together to cover themselves after they realized they were naked in the Garden of Eden?

   a. animal skins

   b. fig leaves

   c. pieces of cloth

   d. palm branches

6. What two things did God put outside the Garden of Eden to block the way to the tree of life?

   a. a gate and a guard

   b. a maze and a river

   c. an angel and a sword

   d. a sphinx and a charm

7. Adam and Eve's first two sons were Cain and Abel.

   a. True

   b. False

8. What food item did Cain present to the Lord as an offering?

   a. fruits of the soil

   b. grain

   c. meat

   d. fat

9. Which descendant of Adam had the longest mortal life in the Bible, and how many years did he live?

   a. Mahalalel, 895 years

   b. Sherupalel, 1,046 years

   c. Enosh, 905 years

   d. Methuselah, 969 years

10. Who of the following was not one of Noah's three sons?

    a. Shem

    b. Joseph

    c. Ham

    d. Japheth

11. Why did God decide to flood the earth in Noah's time?

    a. because of the widespread evil of men

    b. to scatter the people to different places

    c. to save the animals from being destroyed by men

    d. because of global climate factors

12. How many days did the great flood last?

    a. 6

    b. 40

    c. 80

    d. 150

13. How old was Noah when the great flood began?

a. 60

b. 160

c. 330

d. 600

14. After the flood, what was the sign of the covenant between God and humankind, promising he would never again destroy the world with a flood?

    a. a sacrificial lamb

    b. a dove

    c. a rainbow

    d. a burning bush

15. What did God do to the people who were building the Tower of Babel so they would never again try to build "a tower that reaches to the heavens"?

    a. confused their language and dispersed them

    b. struck them down with fire

    c. turned them into pillars of salt

    d. made them all blind

16. God told _____ he would make a great nation from him and cause his descendants to be as numerous as the stars.

    a. Noah

    b. Abraham

    c. Adam

d. Joseph

17. How old were Abraham and Sarah when Sarah became pregnant with their first child?

   a. 80 and 70

   b. 90 and 80

   c. 100 and 90

   d. 110 and 100

18. What was the name of Abraham and Sarah's first child?

   a. Isaac

   b. Jacob

   c. Esau

   d. Joseph

19. Joseph's brothers sold him into slavery. How many brothers did Joseph have?

   a. 10

   b. 11

   c. 12

   d. 13

20. Joseph was thrown into prison because he had an affair with Potiphar's wife.

   a. True

   b. False

21. Joseph's brothers went to Egypt to ask for Joseph's forgiveness.

    a. True

    b. False

22. God destroyed Sodom and Gomorrah by raining down burning sulfur.

    a. True

    b. False

23. Lot's wife turned to sand when she desired to return to Sodom.

    a. True

    b. False

24. What was the name of the baby placed in a basket that floated down the Nile River?

    a. Noah

    b. Joseph

    c. Moses

    d. Aaron

25. God spoke to Moses on Mount Horeb through a
    _____.

    a. burning bush

    b. cloud

    c. parted sea

    d. donkey

26. How many commandments did God give to Moses?

    a. 7

    b. 10

    c. 12

    d. 40

27. Where did Moses go to free the Israelites from slavery?

    a. Israel

    b. Judah

    c. Babylon

    d. Egypt

28. God parted which body of water to allow the Israelites to escape Pharaoh's army?

    a. Mediterranean Sea

    b. Red Sea

    c. Caspian Sea

    d. Sea of Galilee

29. Moses's staff turned into a snake when he threw it to the ground before Pharaoh.

    a. True

    b. False

30. God gave Moses the Ten Commandments on Mount _____.

    a. Horeb

b. Olympus

c. Zion

d. Sinai

31. Moses's father, Amram, lived to be how old?

    a. 125

    b. 137

    c. 149

    d. 161

32. The Israelites were slaves in Egypt for how many years?

    a. 400

    b. 500

    c. 430

    d. 450

33. The first plague cast on Egypt was turning the Nile River into blood.

    a. True

    b. False

34. How did God react after Moses disobeyed his instructions to speak to the rock that would yield water?

    a. promoted Aaron to lead the Israelites

    b. returned Moses to Egypt

    c. told Moses he would never enter the promised land

    d. made Moses a shepherd again

35. How old did men have to be to go to war for Israel?

    a. 16

    b. 18

    c. 20

    d. 21

36. What separated the Most Holy Place from the remainder of the tabernacle?

    a. the chief priest

    b. a curtain

    c. a wailing wall

    d. a pillar of clouds

37. Fire consumed whose sons?

    a. Moses's

    b. Joshua's

    c. Aaron's

    d. Pharaoh's

38. God instructed Moses to speak to a rock that would yield water to the thirsty Israelites while they wandered in the wilderness. What did Moses do instead?

    a. worshipped the rock

    b. struck the rock

    c. condemned the Israelites for their wickedness

    d. cast the rock in the Red Sea

39. What is the first of the Ten Commandments (KJV)?

   a. Thou shalt not murder.

   b. Thou shalt not steal.

   c. Thou shalt not commit adultery.

   d. Thou shalt have no other gods before me.

40. The sixth commandment says you shall not commit adultery.

   a. True

   b. False

41. The ninth commandment says not to give false testimony against your _____.

   a. neighbor

   b. family

   c. spouse

   d. government

42. The promised land was flowing with_____.

   a. milk

   b. priceless jewels

   c. honey

   d. a and c

43. By honoring your father and mother, you may_____.

   a. be rich

b. receive anything you ask for

c. live long

d. live prosperously

44. Deuteronomy is the last book of
   _____.

   a. the Pentateuch

   b. the Major Prophets

   c. the Talmud

   d. wisdom literature

45. Whom did Joshua succeed in leading the Israelite people?

   a. Aaron

   b. Abraham

   c. Moses

   d. Isaac

46. How many times did Joshua and the Israelite army march around Jericho before the city fell to them?

   a. 3

   b. 7

   c. 9

   d. 13

47. When did the Jordan River stop flowing so the Jews could cross it on dry land?

   a. when Joshua slapped the water with his cloak

b. after the next generation of Jews was baptized

c. when the walls of Jericho fell into the river

d. when the feet of those carrying the ark touched the water

48. Who was the first judge of Israel?

a. Caleb

b. Othniel

c. Ehud

d. Deborah

49. Who is the only female judge mentioned in the Bible?

a. Ruth

b. Deborah

c. Hannah

d. Rebekah

50. Samson tied the tails of 400 foxes together, set them on fire, and sent them into the Philistines' wheat fields to destroy their crops.

a. True

b. False

51. Who was Ruth's great-grandson?

a. Saul

b. David

c. Solomon

d. Hezekiah

52. Who was Samuel's father?

   a. Elkanah

   b. Samson

   c. Gideon

   d. none of the above

53. Why did God remove Saul as king and replace him with David?

   a. David was a man after God's own heart.

   b. Saul rejected the word of the Lord.

   c. Saul was an aging king.

   d. David killed Goliath.

54. David killed Goliath with a sling and two stones.

   a. True

   b. False

55. David was the youngest son of _____.

   a. Jesse

   b. Samuel

   c. Saul

   d. Solomon

56. David reigned as king for how many years?

   a. 30

b. 40

c. 50

d. 60

57. While having an affair with Bathsheba, David sent her husband, Uriah, to the front lines of battle so he would be killed.

a. True

b. False

58. Josiah was how many years old when he became king of Israel?

a. 7

b. 8

c. 17

d. 26

59. Besides Elijah, who was the only other person in the Bible never to die?

a. Enoch

b. Elisha

c. Daniel

d. Malachi

60. How many years were God's people in captivity in Babylon?

a. 50

b. 70

c. 80

d. 100

61. David chose _____ to build the house of the Lord in Israel.

    a. Uzziah

    b. Solomon

    c. Jesse

    d. Absalom

62. Solomon asked God for _____.

    a. wealth

    b. mercy

    c. wisdom

    d. peace

63. What two prophets prophesied to the Jews about resuming the building of the temple?

    a. Haggai and Zechariah

    b. Joel and Hosea

    c. Malachi and Zephaniah

    d. Nahum and Habakkuk

64. What was Nehemiah's job at the time of Jerusalem's destruction?

    a. chief official

    b. cupbearer to the king

c. keeper of the king's wardrobe

d. second-in-command

65. Nehemiah organized God's people
to_____.

a. repair the walls of Jerusalem

b. attack the Ammonites

c. attack the Ashdodites

d. rebuild the temple

66. Whose name is never mentioned in the book of Esther?

a. Esther

b. Mordecai

c. God

d. Haman

67. Which king selected Esther to be queen of Persia?

a. Haman

b. Xerxes

c. Josiah

d. Darius

68. As a child, Esther was adopted by her Uncle Mordecai
after her father and mother passed away.

a. True

b. False

69. Job heard God speak to him through a
    _____.

    a. pillar of fire

    b. burning bush

    c. whirlwind

    d. still, small voice

70. Job valued _____ more than anything else in life.

    a. wealth

    b. family

    c. status

    d. the word of the Lord

71. Who authored most of Psalms?

    a. Solomon

    b. David

    c. Paul

    d. none of the above

72. Psalm 119:105 (KJV) says, "Thy word is a lamp unto my feet, and a light unto my _____."

    a. heart

    b. path

    c. eyes

    d. walk

73. Psalm 119 is the longest chapter in the Bible.

    a. True

    b. False

74. Psalm 23 (KJV) opens with, "The Lord is my
    _____; I shall not want."

    a. God

    b. Savior

    c. Shepherd

    d. Redeemer

75. Psalm 119:11 says the author has hidden God's word in his
    heart that he might not sin against God.

    a. True

    b. False

76. Solomon wrote most of the book of Proverbs.

    a. True

    b. False

77. Proverbs 3:5 says, "Trust in the Lord with all your heart,
    soul, mind, and strength."

    a. True

    b. False

78. Proverbs 3:12 says that those the Lord loves, he
    also_____.

    a. blesses

b. strengthens

c. protects

d. disciplines

79. Ecclesiastes 3:1 (KJV) says that "to every thing there is a
_____, and a time to every purpose under the
heaven."

a. reason

b. season

c. truth

d. mission

80. According to Song of Solomon (or Song of Songs) 8:7,
love cannot be quenched by _____.

a. gossip

b. boredom

c. separation

d. many waters

81. Song of Solomon is also known as the Song of Songs.

a. True

b. False

82. Isaiah calls God _____ in Isaiah 12:2 (KJV).

a. Jehovah

b. Jaireh

c. the Great I Am

d. Messiah

83. Isaiah never got the chance to see God in person.

    a. True

    b. False

84. Jeremiah's name means _____.

    a. repent

    b. may Jehovah exalt

    c. child of God

    d. the Lord leads

85. God threatened to turn Jerusalem into a den of _____.

    a. dragons

    b. thieves

    c. lions

    d. doom

86. Lamentations is a _____.

    a. gathering of faith-filled stories

    b. collection of five poems

    c. diary of a despondent prophet

    d. chronology of Old Testament events

87. Ezekiel's mission from God was to _____.

a. warn Israel that foreign nations were about to attack

b. point the Israelites to the coming Messiah

c. proclaim God's message to the Israelites in Babylon

d. bring peace to the Middle East

88. Who gave Ezekiel a scroll to eat?

a. an angel

b. the Lord

c. Ezekiel's father

d. Elijah

89. Where was Daniel sent for praying to God and not to the king?

a. lions' den

b. prison

c. exile

d. Patmos

90. Who protected Shadrach, Meshach, and Abednego in the fiery furnace?

a. the angel Gabriel

b. the hand of God

c. Elijah

d. the Son of God

91. Daniel dreamed of four _____ rising out of

the sea, representing four kingdoms that would eventually succumb to God's kingdom.

a. serpents

b. ships

c. leviathan

d. beasts

92. In Hosea 14:9 (KJV), those who walk in the ways of the Lord are _____.

a. righteous

b. faithful

c. just

d. pure

93. Obadiah is the shortest book in the _____.

a. Old Testament

b. New Testament

c. Bible

d. a and c

94. God told Jonah to go to _____ and warn the people to repent of their sinful ways.

a. Jerusalem

b. Damascus

c. Rome

d. Nineveh

95. Jonah boarded a ship to which city to run away from God?

   a. Bethlehem

   b. Joppa

   c. Tarshish

   d. Jerusalem

96. How was Jonah rescued from drowning in the raging sea?

   a. a passing ship rescued him

   b. Jonah walked on water

   c. a great fish swallowed him

   d. Jonah swam to a deserted island

97. How long did Jonah stay in the belly of the great fish?

   a. 3 days

   b. 7 days

   c. 40 days and 40 nights

   d. overnight

98. Habakkuk is considered one of the 12 Minor Prophets.

   a. True

   b. False

99. Zephaniah was a prophet during the reign of King
   _____.

   a. Uzziah

   b. Josiah

c. Solomon

d. Jeroboam

100. The second chapter of Malachi is the last chapter of the Old Testament.

a. True

b. False

New Testament Questions

1. Quoting the prophet Isaiah, Matthew tells us that one name for Jesus will be Immanuel, which means _____.

   a. God reigns

   b. God saves

   c. God with us

   d. God for us

2. Which of the following were not one of the three things the devil tempted Jesus to do before Jesus began his public ministry?

   a. turn stones to bread

   b. jump off a building

   c. worship the devil

   d. walk on water

3. According to Jesus, the wise man builds his house on _____, while the fool builds his house on _____.

   a. rock; sand

   b. foundation; swamp

   c. his word; falsehood

   d. God; Satan

4. Jesus says the kingdom of heaven is like _____.

a. a mustard seed

b. an olive tree

c. a wonderful party

d. a camel's eye

5. The traditional names of three magi (wise men) who visited the baby Jesus are Balthazar, Melchior, and Caspar.

a. True

b. False

6. What was the name of Jesus's stepfather?

a. Nicodemus

b. Simon

c. Caiaphas

d. Joseph

7. Mary and Joseph were married when Jesus was born.

a. True

b. False

8. What was Matthew's occupation prior to becoming a disciple?

a. fisherman

b. shepherd

c. innkeeper

d. tax collector

9. Who told Mary and Joseph to take Jesus and flee to another country when Jesus was a young boy?

    a. Herod

    b. the magi

    c. John the Baptist

    d. an angel of the Lord

10. After Jesus was baptized, God's Spirit descended from heaven in the form of an eagle.

    a. True

    b. False

11. Jesus was baptized by_____.

    a. John the Baptist

    b. Joseph

    c. Nicodemus

    d. the Sanhedrin

12. How did King Herod kill John the Baptist?

    a. crucifixion

    b. lions' den

    c. fiery furnace

    d. beheading

13. How many men did Jesus feed using just five loaves of bread and two fish?

a. 4,000

b. 5,000

c. 6,000

d. 7,000

14. How long did Jesus fast in the desert?

    a. 7 days

    b. 30 days

    c. 40 days

    d. 60 days

15. Who betrayed Jesus and got him arrested?

    a. Judas

    b. Caiaphas

    c. Peter

    d. Thomas

16. When Jesus was arrested, one of his disciples reacted by cutting off an ear of the high priest's slave with a sword.

    a. True

    b. False

17. How many times did Peter deny knowing Jesus when someone identified him as a disciple in the courtyard?

    a. once

    b. twice

c. three times

d. four times

18. From the sixth hour to the ninth hour, as Jesus hung on the cross, there was _____ over the land.

a. darkness

b. a thunderstorm

c. mourning

d. an earthquake

19. _____ committed suicide before Jesus's resurrection.

a. Caiaphas

b. Bartholomew

c. Peter

d. Judas

20. Tax collectors like Matthew were among the most popular people in Jewish society.

a. True

b. False

21. Jesus told Peter to forgive someone _____.

a. 70 x 7 times

b. 70 times

c. 7 times

d. 325 times

22. Jesus said the two greatest commandments are to love God with all your heart, soul, mind, and strength and to love your neighbor as yourself.

    a. True

    b. False

23. Where was Jesus baptized?

    a. Nile River

    b. Jordan River

    c. Sea of Galilee

    d. Sistine Chapel

24. The disciples John and _____ were brothers.

    a. Peter

    b. Andrew

    c. Matthew

    d. James

25. In Matthew 8, Jesus was _____ as the disciples took a boat across a lake.

    a. praying

    b. teaching

    c. sleeping

    d. walking on water

26. What did Jesus do when a raging storm shook the boat he was in?

    a. rebuked and calmed the storm

    b. prayed for wisdom

    c. walked on water

    d. rebuked the disciples' lack of faith

27. Who believed that Jesus was John the Baptist?

    a. Caiaphas

    b. Pilate

    c. Herod

    d. Nicodemus

28. John the Baptist was Jesus's uncle.

    a. True

    b. False

29. The first two disciples whom Jesus called were
    _____.

    a. James and John

    b. Thomas and Bartholomew

    c. Matthew and Judas

    d. Peter and Andrew

30. The disciples James and John were the sons of
    _____.

a. Zebedee

b. Zechariah

c. Zacchaeus

d. Zephaniah

31. Jesus said the Sabbath was made for _____.

a. God's glory

b. man

c. rest

d. worship

32. Who of the following was not one of Jesus's 12 disciples?

a. Bartholomew

b. Thaddaeus

c. Matthias

d. Philip

33. Jesus said the kingdom of God is like a _____.

a. vine and branches

b. house built on a rock

c. little child

d. mustard seed

34. After Jesus fed thousands of people by the Sea of Galilee, the disciples picked up how many basketfuls of leftover bread and fish?

a. 5

b. 7

c. 12

d. 40

35. What did Jesus do to heal the blind man at Bethsaida?

    a. spit on his eyes and put his hands on them

    b. poured water over his eyes

    c. a and b

    d. none of the above

36. Who appeared to Jesus, Peter, James, and John at the transfiguration?

    a. Abraham

    b. Elijah

    c. Moses

    d. b and c

37. Which current holiday commemorates Jesus's triumphant donkey ride into Jerusalem, to adoring crowds?

    a. Easter

    b. Good Friday

    c. Palm Sunday

    d. Maundy Thursday

38. Though he doesn't identify himself in the book, who do many people consider to be the author of Mark's Gospel?

   a. John Mark

   b. Matthew

   c. Luke

   d. John

39. Jeremiah is the first prophet quoted in Mark.

   a. True

   b. False

40. Jesus told believers who wanted to come after him to deny themselves, take up their _____, and follow him.

   a. cross

   b. burdens

   c. prayers

   d. innermost being

41. What is the name of the angel who announced to Mary that she would conceive the "Son of the Most High"?

   a. Michael

   b. David

   c. Raphael

   d. Gabriel

42. What are the names of the two righteous people who celebrated the presentation of the baby Jesus?

a. Simeon and Anna

b. Phanuel and Elizabeth

c. Simon and Ananias

d. Zacchaeus and Sapphira

43. John the Baptist considered himself unworthy to do what for Jesus?

a. baptize him

b. kiss his feet

c. untie his sandals

d. be baptized by him

44. What afflicted the man whose friends lowered him into a house to be healed by Jesus?

a. blindness

b. leprosy

c. paralysis

d. gout

45. According to Luke's Gospel, which of these disciples' names is not shared by another apostle?

a. John

b. Simon

c. Judas

d. James

46. Who was the first to learn the news of Jesus's birth?

    a. high priests

    b. Caesar Augustus

    c. shepherds

    d. none of the above

47. When the shepherds visited Jesus, he was in a
    _____.

    a. home

    b. stable

    c. palace

    d. temple

48. The shepherds found Jesus wrapped in _____.

    a. a manger

    b. donkey saddle blankets

    c. camel hair

    d. swaddling clothes

49. Jesus's hometown was _____.

    a. Nazareth

    b. Galilee

    c. Bethlehem

    d. Capernaum

50. Jesus began his public ministry at about age
   _____.

   a. 18

   b. 21

   c. 30

   d. 33

51. "Blessed are you who weep now, for you will laugh" is one
   of the _____ that Jesus taught.

   a. sermons on the Mount

   b. Beatitudes

   c. parables

   d. homilies

52. The parable of the good Samaritan taught a lesson on how
   to treat your _____.

   a. family

   b. work associates

   c. neighbor

   d. spouse

53. On the Sabbath, Jesus healed a man suffering from
   _____.

   a. leprosy

   b. demon possession

c. blindness

d. dropsy

54. According to John, Jesus Christ, the Word of God, is full of grace and _____.

    a. mercy

    b. power

    c. truth

    d. sacrifice

55. Jesus instructed the woman at the well to give him _____.

    a. bread

    b. water

    c. faith

    d. a denarius

56. When John the Baptist saw Jesus, he said, "Look, _____ who takes away the sin of the world!"

    a. the Son of God

    b. the Son of Man

    c. the Lamb of God

    d. the Messiah

57. Jesus's first miracle recorded in John's Gospel was _____.

    a. turning water into wine at a wedding

b. healing a blind man

c. walking on water

d. driving out demons

58. Jesus told Nicodemus that no one could see the kingdom of God unless they were _____.

a. following him

b. devoted to God

c. perfect

d. born again

59. Who provided the five small barley loaves and two fish that Jesus turned into food for thousands of men, women, and children?

a. Andrew

b. Peter

c. a boy

d. a local fish market

60. What did Jesus tell the woman caught in adultery?

a. "Go now and leave your life of sin."

b. "Let any one of you who is without sin be the first to throw a stone at her."

c. "Your sins are forgiven."

d. "You must be born again."

61. Which of the following titles did Jesus not give to himself?

a. the gate for the sheep

b. the Good Shepherd

c. the chief of chiefs

d. I am

62. How long was Lazarus in a tomb before Jesus raised him from the dead?

a. 1 day

b. 2 days

c. 3 days

d. 4 days

63. Caiaphas, the high priest, led the plot to kill Jesus.

a. True

b. False

64. Jesus said he is the _____.

a. truth

b. way

c. life

d. all the above

65. At the Last Supper, Jesus told Peter that _____ he would deny Jesus _____.

a. before Jesus died; four times

b. before the rooster crowed; three times

c. before Jesus died; three times

d. before the rooster crowed; four times

66. On the night Jesus was betrayed, he prayed _____.

   a. for all believers

   b. for his disciples

   c. to be glorified

   d. all the above

67. Where was Jesus arrested?

   a. in the upper room

   b. in a garden

   c. in the temple

   d. in a courtyard

68. Who handed Jesus to the Jewish officials to be crucified?

   a. Pilate

   b. Annas

   c. Caiaphas

   d. Herod

69. Pilate had a notice prepared and fastened to the cross. It read: Jesus of Nazareth, _____.

   a. Lord of lords

   b. a common criminal

c. the King of the Jews

d. the Savior of the world

70. Who was the only disciple who saw Jesus's crucifixion, according to the book of John?

a. Peter

b. James

c. Matthew

d. John

71. What were Jesus's final words before dying?

a. "My God, my God, why have you forsaken me?"

b. "It is finished."

c. "Father, forgive them, for they do not know what they are doing."

d. "Into your hands I commit my spirit."

72. Who asked Pilate for Jesus's body after he died?

a. Joseph of Arimathea

b. Nicodemus

c. Mary

d. John

73. Mary Magdalene was the first person to notice that Jesus's tomb was empty on the third day (after his crucifixion).

a. True

b. False

74. Which two disciples saw Jesus's empty tomb?

    a. Peter and John

    b. James and John

    c. Andrew and John

    d. Peter and Andrew

75. Mary, Jesus's mother, was the first person to see Jesus after his resurrection.

    a. True

    b. False

76. Which disciple was not around when Jesus first appeared to them?

    a. Peter

    b. Thomas

    c. Philip

    d. Bartholomew

77. Jesus told Thomas to touch his hands and his side so he would stop doubting and believe.

    a. True

    b. False

78. On what Jewish holiday did the Holy Spirit come upon the disciples?

    a. Pentecost

    b. Passover

c. Feast of Booths

d. Christmas

79. Saul was on the road to _____ when he saw a great light, and the Lord spoke to him and temporarily blinded him.

a. Jerusalem

b. Damascus

c. Ephesus

d. Arabia

80. Who wrote the book of Acts?

a. Paul

b. Barnabas

c. Luke

d. Peter

81. Who replaced Judas among the disciples?

a. Paul

b. Luke

c. Barnabas

d. Matthias

82. Who freed Peter from jail after he was arrested by Herod?

a. John

b. The Romans

c. an angel

d. Paul

83. Romans 3:23 says that "all have sinned and fall short of
_____."

   a. God's perfect standards

   b. fulfilling God's plans

   c. earning entrance into heaven

   d. the glory of God

84. Romans 5:8 teaches that God demonstrates his own
love for us in that, while we were still sinners, Christ
_____.

   a. died for us

   b. was praying for us in heaven

   c. offered us eternal life

   d. came to earth as a baby

85. Romans 6:23 says that the wages of sin is
_____, but the gift of God is _____
in Christ Jesus our Lord.

   a. trouble on earth; approval

   b. hell; eternal life

   c. death; salvation

   d. death; eternal life

86. According to the book of Romans, most authority is
established by God.

a. True

b. False

87. Who is the father of many nations?

   a. Abraham

   b. Adam

   c. David

   d. Peter

88. The book of Romans is considered _____.

   a. an epistle

   b. a history book

   c. a love letter

   d. an allegory

89. First Corinthians 13 is commonly known as the
   _____ chapter.

   a. faith

   b. love

   c. discipleship

   d. evangelism

90. Galatians 3:23 tells Christians that whatever they do, they
   should do it with all their heart, as they are working for
   _____.

   a. the kingdom of God

   b. the Lord

c. the gospel

d. their church

91. We become children of God by faith in Jesus Christ.

   a. True

   b. False

92. Which of the following is not part of the fruit of the Spirit?

   a. joy

   b. patience

   c. goodness

   d. tolerance

93. How are people saved, according to Ephesians 2:8-9?

   a. by grace through faith

   b. by good works

   c. by a mix of grace and good works

   d. by a mix of faith and good works

94. Ephesians 5:25 instructs that husbands should love their wives _____.

   a. as they love themselves

   b. with an everlasting love

   c. to the degree that their wives love them

   d. as Christ loved the church

95. In Philippians 4:13, Paul says he can do all things through
_____, who gives him strength.

   a. his inner resources

   b. Christ

   c. the Holy Spirit

   d. faith

96. Philippians 2:6-7 references Jesus taking the form of a
_____ when he left heaven and came to earth as
a man.

   a. baby

   b. holy man

   c. prophet

   d. servant

97. According to Philippians, Jesus is the name above every
other name.

   a. True

   b. False

98. Colossians 3:23 states that whatever we do, we
should work at it with all our heart, as working for
_____.

   a. our family

   b. the Lord

   c. the church

   d. other gods

99. _____ is being sure of what we hope for and certain of what we do not see, according to Hebrews 11:1.

    a. faith

    b. love

    c. heaven

    d. discernment

100. James informs us that faith without good works is _____.

    a. dead

    b. incomplete

    c. still valuable

    d. faith alone

Answer Key

General Bible Answers

1. c

2. b

3. d

4. d

5. b

6. b

7. a

8. c

9. c

10. a

11. e

12. b

13. c

14. a

15. d

16. a

17. a

18. a

19. b (**Correct answer:** the books of Daniel and Revelation)

20. c

Old Testament Answers

1. c

2. d

3. b (**Correct answer:** God told them not to eat from this tree.)

4. c

5. b

6. c

7. a

8. a

9. d

10. b

11. a

12. b

13. d

14. c

15. a

16. b

17. c

18. a

19. b (**Correct answer:** Joseph had 11 brothers.)

20. b (**Correct answer:** Potiphar's wife falsely accused him of rape.)

21. b (**Correct answer:** to buy grain)

22. a

23. b (**Correct answer:** a pillar of salt)

24. c

25. a

26. b

27. d

28. b

29. b (**Correct Answer:** Aaron threw down the staff.)

30. d

31. b

32. c

33. a

34. c

35. c

36. b

37. c

38. b

39. d

40. b (**Correct answer:** The sixth commandment is "Thou shalt not murder.")

41. a

42. d

43. c

44. a

45. c

46. d

47. d

48. b

49. b

50. b (**Correct answer:**
300 foxes)

51. b

52. a

53. b

54. b (**Correct answer:**
sling and one stone)

55. a

56. b

57. a

58. b

59. a

60. b

61. b

62. c

63. a

64. b

65. a

66. c

67. b

68. b (**Correct answer:**
She was Mordecai's
cousin.)

69. c

70. d

71. b

72. b

73. a

74. c

75. a

76. a

77. b (**Correct answer:**
"Trust in the
LORD with all your
heart and lean
not on your own
understanding.")

78. d

79. b

80. d

81. a

82. a

83. b (**Correct answer:**
Isaiah saw the Lord
in the year that
King Uzziah died.)

84. b

85. a

86. b

87. c

88. b

89. a

90. d

91. d

92. c

93. a

94. d

95. c

96. c

97. a

98. a

99. b

100. b (**Correct Answer:** Malachi has four chapters.)

New Testament Answers

1. c

2. d

3. a

4. a

5. a

6. d

7. a

8. d

9. d

10. b (**Correct answer:** in the form of a dove)

11. a

12. d

13. b

14. c

15. a

16. a

17. c

18. a

19. d

20. b (**Correct Answer:** least popular)

21. a

22. a

23. b

24. d

25. c

26. a

27. c

28. b (**Correct answer:** cousin)

29. d

30. a

31. b

32. c

33. d

34. c

35. a

36. d

37. c

38. a

39. b (**Correct answer:** Isaiah)

40. a

41. d

42. a

43. c

44. c

45. a

46. c

47. b

48. d

49. a

50. c

51. b

52. c

53. d

54. c

55. b

56. c

57. a

58. d

59. c

60. a

61. c

62. d

63. a

64. d

65. b

66. d

67. b

68. a

69. c

70. d

71. b

72. a

73. a

74. a

75. b (**Correct answer:** Mary Magdalene was the first.)

76. b

77. a

78. a

79. b

80. c

81. d

82. c

83. d

84. a

85. d

86. b (**Correct answer:** all authority)

87. a

88. a

89. b

90. b

91. a

92. d

93. a

94. d

95. b

96. d

97. a

98. b

99. a

100. a

PART 4

Essential Bible
Verses

Essential Bible Verses

The Beginnings
- Genesis 1:1
- John 1:1
- John 1:14
- John 3:16

The Great Commission
- Matthew 28:18-20
- Acts 1:8

The Plan of Salvation
- Romans 3:23
- Romans 5:8
- Romans 6:23
- Romans 10:9-10

The Word of God and Prayer
- Deuteronomy 6:6-7
- Joshua 1:8
- Psalm 119:11
- 2 Timothy 3:16
- Hebrews 4:12
- Hebrews 4:16
- 1 John 5:14-15

Assurance
- Psalm 23
- Isaiah 26:3

- Isaiah 53:5-6
- John 14:1-3
- John 14:6
- John 14:27
- 1 John 5:11-12

Praise and Adoration

- Psalm 100:4-5
- 1 Peter 1:3
- Revelation 4:11

God's Promises

- Proverbs 3:5-6
- Jeremiah 29:11
- Matthew 6:33
- Romans 8:28
- 1 Corinthians 10:13
- 1 Peter 5:7
- 1 John 1:7
- 1 John 1:9

Instructions in Christian Living

- 2 Chronicles 7:14
- Proverbs 1:7
- Proverbs 15:1
- Romans 12:1-2
- Romans 12:11-12
- Romans 12:18
- 2 Corinthians 9:7
- Hebrews 10:25

Faith and Trust in God
- Psalm 4:8
- Psalm 56:3
- Romans 1:16-17
- Galatians 2:20
- Ephesians 2:8-10
- Hebrews 11:6

The Fullness of the Holy Spirit
- Galatians 5:16-18
- Ephesians 5:18-20

Pure Joy
- Psalm 118:24
- Philippians 4:4-7
- 1 Thessalonians 5:16-18
- James 1:2-4

The First and Second Comings of Christ
- Isaiah 9:6
- Luke 2:10-12
- Acts 1:11
- James 5:7-8
- Revelation 22:20

About the General Editor

Stan Toler has spoken in more than 90 countries and written more than 100 books with sales of more than 3 million copies. Toler for many years served as vice president and instructor for John C. Maxwell's INJOY Leadership Institute, training leaders to make a difference in the world. Maxwell calls Toler "Mister Relationship." He says, "Stan Toler has the uncanny ability to see the humor in any situation, capture it in his imagination, and then recount it with the grace and style of a southern storyteller."

More than one million registrants have been inspired and entertained by his speaking and teaching. Renowned motivational speaker Zig Ziglar said of Toler, "He teaches principles and procedures that will build a church, a home, a business, a community, or a nation."

To learn more about Harvest House books and
to read sample chapters, visit our website:

www.harvesthousepublishers.com

HARVEST HOUSE PUBLISHERS
EUGENE, OREGON